The Rise Of Mr. Ponzi

by

Charles Ponzi

For historical accuracy from original manuscript:

CHARLES PONZI, *Publisher*
New York City
Via Bormida 2
Rome, Italy

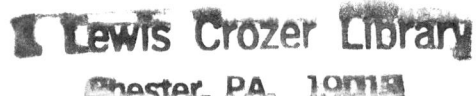

The Rise
Of Mr. Ponzi

U.S. Edition

© *Portions of this book are copyright protected*
Copyright 2001 by Inkwell Publishers, Ltd.

7009 Kiwi Place
Naples, Fl. 34113
(941) 417-9545

Mmathosian@aol.com or Mmath4@cs.com

While reasonable efforts have been taken in preparation of this book to assure its accuracy; the editor/publisher assumes no liability resulting from any errors or omissions in this book or from the use of information contained herein.

Library of Congress card number in process

ISBN – 0-9631924-4-2

Printed in the United States of America
All rights reserved
Reproduction by any means prohibited
History, Crime, Biography

CONTENTS

	Introduction – Meet Mr. Ponzi! The Champion Get-Rich-Quick Wallingford Of America xii
I	Mr. Ponzi Lands In Boston With $2.50 To Add A $15,000,000 Chapter To The History Of State Street Finance 1
II	Mr. Ponzi Bobs Up In Montreal With One Dollar And Buys Himself A Peck Of Trouble 6
III	Mr. Ponzi Falls From The Frying Pan Into The Fire And Wonders What It Is All About 10
IV	By Adding Two And Two Together, Mr. Ponzi Develops An Analytic Mind And Arrives At The Inevitable Hour 17
V	Uncle Sam, In The Person Of An Immigration Inspector, Plays A Dirty Trick On Mr. Ponzi 23
VI	Mr. Ponzi Swaps a 2' x 4' County Jail For Uncle Sam's $10,000,000 Big-House 29
VII	"Page Mr. Insull!" Or The Ponzi Power, Light & Water Company of Blockton, Ala 33
VIII	Mr. Ponzi's Medical Career In Mobile Is Abruptly Cut Short By A University President 39
IX	Mr. Ponzi Pulls A Fast One On The New Orleans Citizenry And Ducks None Too Soon 44

X	From the Copious Crop Of American Blossoms Mr. Ponzi Picks Himself An Exquisite Rose Of The American Beauty Variety As His Life's Emblem	51
XI	School Street, Boston, Scene Of The Explosion That Was Heard Around The World	56
XII	Mr. Ponzi Promotes "The Trader's Guide" With A 3,000,000 Circulation Right Off The Bat	61
XIII	Mr. Ponzi Finally Discovers An Untrodden Path To Fabulous Wealth And Takes It	67
XIV	Mr. Ponzi Organizes The Securities Exchange Company On The Pattern Of A One-Man-Band	71
XV	Mr. Ponzi's Life Becomes One Nightmare Of Police And Postal Inspectors	77
XVI	Mr. Ponzi Disproves The Theory That There Cannot Be A Profit Without A Corresponding Loss	82
XVII	Mr. Ponzi Opines That, If Gambling Is A Sin, He'd Better Have The Church On His Side	89
XVIII	Mr. Ponzi Takes It Into His Head To Clean Up A Few Banks Without Dutch Cleanser	96
XIX	Mr. Ponzi Goes Shopping And Buys A Million Dollars Worth Of Sunday Parcels	104
XX	Mr. Ponzi, Heading For The Rocks, Manages To Steer Clear Of Them For A While	113

XXI	Ladies Stop "Runs" With Lux, But Mr. Ponzi Stops One With A Million Dollars 121
XXII	Mr. Ponzi, Peeved At The "Money Lenders" Declares War On Them And Begins Hostilities . . 127
XXIII	Mr. Ponzi Offers Uncle Sam $200,000,000 For His Shipping Board Fleet 135
XXIV	Mr. Ponzi Is Fifteen Million Bucks Ahead Of Game But Does Not Quit 144
XXV	The Battle Royal Is On, With The Odds In Favor Of Mr. Ponzi 151
XXVI	Oh, Boy! What A Fight! The Fur Is Still Flying And You Can't Tell Which Is Which! 159
XXVII	A Couple Of Windjammers Settle Mr. Ponzi's Goose And He Goes Down For The Count Of Ten! 165

Preface.....

Ponzi scheme (pon ze) n. An investment swindle in which high profits are promised from fictitious sources and early investors are paid off with funds raised from later ones. [After *Charles Ponzi* (1882? - 1949), Italian-born speculator.]
© *The American Heritage College Dictionary, Third Edition*

Meet Charles Ponzi, The Financial Wizard Of Boston

Before reading Mr. Ponzi's autobiography, it will be worth your while to read this introduction about the man, his scheme and his demise. Why? Because Ponzi's version of his life story and events surrounding his get-rich-quick scheme may be dramatically different than the same story told by someone else, say, one of his fraud victims or an auditor who investigated his books and records.

As you might expect, Ponzi paints a rosy portrait of himself and his past. He writes a somewhat glamorous rendition of his life story and his get-rich-quick scheme. You may also find it interesting, as I did, that Ponzi titled his book, "The Rise of Mr. Ponzi." Nowhere in the title is there reference to the *fall* of Mr. Ponzi, and fall he did!

To help you better understand the man and his 'Ponzi scheme,' I gathered information about his life and criminal activities as documented through Ponzi's own testimony, historical records and investigative news reporting. Included in this summary is a synopsis of Ponzi's arrest history in Canada and the United States. Unfortunately, information about Ponzi's life in Italy, before he came to America, is sketchy. It is alleged he was a petty criminal and at best an unethical person. Regardless of what people say about, or call Mr. Ponzi, his autobiography is an interesting and absorbing read! A real page-turner, as they say. Does he always tell the truth? You be the judge.

COMING TO AMERICA

Ponzi was born in Italy in 1882. He lived in Italy until age twenty-one when he hitched a ride to America on a steam ship, the SS. Vancouver. Like thousands of European immigrants before him, he came to America to fulfill his dreams of riches and fame.

It is believed that Ponzi learned to speak English while working as a dishwasher in a New York restaurant. He was later promoted to waiter. It has also been reported that Ponzi was caught short changing bills at this same restaurant and that his career as a waiter ended abruptly.

In 1907 he made his way to Montreal, Canada, and became employed as an assistant teller at an international bank. As an assistant bank teller, Ponzi had access to customer records and he took advantage of his easy access to the money. Ponzi forged a customer's signature on bank checks and stole the money. He was convicted of forgery and in 1908 he was sentenced to three years in a Canadian prison. When he committed this crime Ponzi was using the alias Charles Bianchi. After his release from prison Ponzi returned to America. He headed back to the U.S. by railway. However, he was not alone on the train. Ponzi was accompanied by a small group of Italian immigrants who could speak little or no English and who didn't have proper immigration papers. Ponzi was charged with smuggling illegal aliens across the border and once again was sent to prison. This time he was incarcerated in a prison in Atlanta, Georgia. After serving about two years he was released. He then headed to Boston, Massachusetts.

In Boston, Ponzi found employment as a low level clerk for the J. P. Poole Import - Export Firm. It was around this time that Ponzi became familiar with an instrument that would be the basis for his future investment scam - *international postal reply coupons*.

THE SCHEME IS HATCHED

In 1907 an International Postal Congress decided to issue postal reply coupons around the world. These coupons could be redeemed for postage stamps in the participating countries. Relatives and friends in America, who could afford it, would buy and mail the postal reply coupons to friends and family in Europe. Those receiving the coupons would redeem them for stamps in their own post office. The stamps could then be used as postage on envelopes mailed back to family and friends in America.

During the early 1900's Europe was suffering from a severe case of inflation and depression. The United States economy was strong and growing. As a result, U.S. dollars were more valuable than the currency issued by other countries participating in the international postal reply coupon program.

Ponzi figured that if someone in Europe exchanged American dollars for currency of their own country they could buy postal reply coupons at their post office at a better rate. He believed that someone could buy coupons in Europe, send them to him in America and he could replace the coupons for U.S. stamps of a higher value. He could then sell these stamps at a small discount to generate cash. Using the Italian lira as an example, Ponzi explains the transaction in his autobiography like this:

"…It [the lira] was quoted then about 5 cents instead of 20 cents. One lira was equal to 100 centesimi. With 2,000 centesimi I could have obtained 66 coupons at 30 centesimi each. Or enough coupons to obtain in exchange for them at the Boston post-office $3.30 of 5 cent stamps. A gross profit of 230%."

Ponzi calculated that by taking advantage of the international exchange rates, he could make huge profits on the coupons-for-stamps transactions. He would then purchase more coupons with his profits and cash those in thereby generating even higher returns. Ponzi believed that by playing the international markets in this fashion he could pyramid his profits into millions. Convinced he had discovered a 'no lose' formula for success, Ponzi promoted this idea to anyone and everyone. He believed he had identified a legitimate way to make big profits at the governments' expense.

With a smile on his face, and the self-confidence of a con man, Ponzi offered everyone he spoke with the opportunity to get in on his investment venture. He promised investors a return of 50% in 45 days or double your investment if you were willing to invest your money for up to 3 months. He assured everyone that these huge returns were realistic because he was making such huge profits on the trading of international postal reply coupons.

PONZI GOES PUBLIC

With much enthusiasm about his investment concept, Ponzi decided to start his own business. In November of 1919, he established the *Securities Exchange Company* (SEC) at 27 School Street in downtown Boston. He started his business on a shoestring. In fact, to furnish his new business Ponzi borrowed all of his furniture from a business associate named J. R. Daniels.

In the beginning, a few daring Bostonians loaned him money and in return Ponzi issued them promissory notes. When the promissory notes matured, Ponzi paid the investors as promised. Word spread quickly! Friends, business associates and families of those first investors wanted in on the action. Within weeks Ponzi became so busy that he had to hire sales associates to help him sell the promissory note investments. The lobby of Ponzi's small office on School Street became busier than the lobbies of the larger local banks. In fact, bank depositors were withdrawing their savings and turning the cash over to Ponzi for investment. Why the run on the banks? Because the banks were paying a measly 4-5% on savings deposits. Sign up with Ponzi and you would receive a promissory note for your original amount plus a guaranteed return of 50 to 100% interest in 45 or 90 days. And, when your note came due, you could roll your investment over and earn even more money.

Policemen, priests, mothers, blue-collar workers, everyone was investing. The money poured into the office of the SEC. Ponzi became so busy that he hired off duty policemen to maintain law and order in the streets outside of his office and to carry large satchels of cash to his banks on regular intervals throughout the day. He also hired a score of commissioned sales representatives and opened up branch offices outside of Boston and in other states.

Within months Ponzi received about $3.5 million from investors. He owed those same investors a whopping $4.5 million in interest and principal, but he continued to redeem his SEC notes as they came due.

PONZI BUYS A BANK

By May 1920, more than one thousand investors purchased Ponzi's promissory notes. He quickly gained fame and notoriety and was referred to by many as the "Financial Wizard" of Boston, a modern day Midas, the man with the golden touch. Ponzi recognized his growing notoriety and took full advantage of it. In fact, while the money poured in he began plotting a new scheme. A scheme that involved the takeover of a Boston bank – the Hanover Trust Bank.

Ponzi started depositing thousands of dollars into an account at the Hanover Trust Bank in Boston. Ponzi figured that once he had enough money in the bank to be considered the "largest depositor," he could put the squeeze on bank management to make him head of the bank. He surmised that if they refused to do that he would threaten to withdraw his money and the bank would collapse. His threats worked! Ponzi manipulated his way into Hanover and by the summer of 1920, he secured a controlling interest by purchasing $3 million in bank stock. In the meantime Ponzi's SEC business grew wildly.

PONZI BECOMES THE PIED PIPER OF BOSTON

As the Securities Exchange Company prospered, so did Ponzi. He was living the big life. He purchased a huge 20-room house just outside of Boston for $100,000 and equipped it with air conditioning, heat and a heated pool. He buzzed around town in a $12,000 chauffer driven automobile and could be seen on any day, dapperly dressed in a business suit and toting a gold handled malacca walking cane. He brought his mother over from Italy and hired a publicity man, William McMasters, to handle the media attention he was receiving. He also used some of the proceeds from the SEC investments to purchase the J.P. Poole Import-Export Firm and immediately fired his old boss.

Within six months of opening his business Ponzi emerged, undeniably the hero of the little man, the small investor, so overlooked by the existing banking establishment. Like the Pied Piper, everywhere Ponzi went his fans were sure to follow. Even later on, when his money-making abilities were being challenged, his fans stuck by him. A well-publicized interaction with one of his followers that occurred while Ponzi stood on the steps of the State House before a crowd in Boston, went something like this:

"You're the greatest Italian of all," yelled an admirer.

"Oh, no," replied Ponzi. "Columbus and Marconi." Columbus discovered America. Marconi discovered the wireless."

"Sure, but you discovered money!" yelled the man.

THE NEWSPAPERS TAKE NOTICE

During the early stages of his scam, Ponzi's credibility was actually boosted by an article that was published in the local newspaper.

The Boston Post (*The Post*) ran a story on July 24, 1920, that profiled Ponzi and his money making prowess. It described his postal reply coupon program and reported that he "doubles the money within three months." The story highlighted the fact that Ponzi promised a return of "50% in 45 days, 100 percent in 90 days, on any amount invested." It also reported that, "Even government officials sent to investigate him have wound up by investing with him." As icing on the cake *The Post* also reported that "...the authorities have not been able to discover a single illegal thing about it."

As a result of this media exposure, a small run on the offices of the SEC began. Investors clamored at the doors of the SEC trying to get in on this excellent investment opportunity! Then, as luck would have it, another article appeared which seemed to turn the tide of investors.

Kinks in Ponzi's armor started to appear when J.R. Daniels, the person who loaned Ponzi furniture to start the SEC, came forward and accused Ponzi of owing him $1.5 million. Daniels sued Ponzi, alleging that he was Ponzi's partner and that he was entitled to, but never received, any of the profits from the operation of the SEC. Daniel's lawsuit brought more media attention to Ponzi and raised eyebrows when people asked why, if Ponzi was so rich, was he 'renting furniture?' *The Post* started publishing more articles about Ponzi and those articles raised interesting issues and questions. More runs on the SEC began. However, this time people wanted their money back.

Ponzi gladly gave back the money with a smile on his face. He redeemed promissory notes for days. Knowing something about human nature, Ponzi figured that if he gave complaining investors their money back, eventually the run would stop and confidence in him would be restored. In fact, that is exactly what happened. When people realized he was able to refund their money, the run on the SEC stopped. Investor funds once again poured in. However, the article in *The Post* raised hard questions that begged answers. The news coverage sparked the inquisitive nature of officials from the Commission of Banks and the Boston office of the Attorney General.

Representatives from those organizations made a visit to Ponzi's office and asked him to kindly explain how he was able to reap such large profits from International Postal Reply Coupons. Ponzi explained his program to the men and offered to allow an audit of the books and records of the SEC. In his self-assured manner, Ponzi promised the officials he would stop taking in any new deposits while the audit was conducted, but would continue to pay interest to his existing investors and redeem existing notes when presented. By now, after eight months of operation, Ponzi claimed to have made almost $10 million juggling international postal reply coupons.

THE BUBBLE BEGINS TO CRACK

In a July 27, 1920 issue of *The Post* an article appeared titled, "PONZI CLOSES; NOT LIKELY TO RESUME." Ponzi is quoted as saying the following about the audit and his office operation:

"I have made a personal agreement with District Attorney Pelletier to close receiving funds from the public for investments with the Securities Exchange Company…and all branches until after an official audit is made to determine my solvency and satisfy him that my methods of financial operation are thoroughly legitimate."

He goes on to state, "Meantime, I shall pay all maturing obligations as presented."

Per their agreement, the SEC remained open while the audit proceeded. In the meantime Ponzi hatched his next scheme. He would attempt to convince the Board of Directors of the Hanover Trust Bank to give him $10 million to purchase a fleet of retired U.S. merchant ships from the U.S. government.

Ponzi's plan was to 'transfer' all investment assets and liabilities of the SEC operation to the new business and allow SEC investors to exchange promissory notes for stock in the new venture. What people didn't realize was that Ponzi was trying to legitimatize his illegal investment business. To use today's terminology, Ponzi was trying to launder his illegally gotten gains through a legitimate business, thereby covering up the fraud he was perpetrating. However, the bankers said, "No!"

From July through August 1920, *The Post* continued publishing a slew of negative investigative reports about Ponzi and his business. To further their inquiry, the newspaper contacted Clarence Barron, of the famed Barron financial empire, and asked him to critique Ponzi's operation. One of the first questions Barron asked (paraphrased) was, if Ponzi is able to make so much money with his postal coupon program, then why is he "investing his money in banks!?" A valid question, no doubt.

On August 2, 1920, *The Post* dropped another bombshell when it reported on the front page of the newspaper, "DECLARES PONZI IS NOW HOPELESSLY INSOLVENT." Under the headline in big, bold letters the article reported, "Publicity Expert Employed by "Wizard" Says He Has Not Sufficient Funds to Meet His Notes – States He Has Sent No Money to Europe Nor Received Money From Europe Recently."

William McMasters, Ponzi's public relations man, wrote the expose. In the article McMasters reported that Ponzi was over $2 million in debt "even if he tried to meet his notes without paying any interest." McMasters also reported that by Ponzi's own admission he had not sent a dollar abroad or received a dollar from abroad for the past 60 days. After ripping into Ponzi and the operation of the SEC throughout the entire article, McMasters blatantly states, "on Saturday, I reached the conclusion – after developments of a week – that he was hopelessly insolvent."

On August 10, 1920, government officials seized all of Ponzi's books and records.

BIANCHI, THE SNAKE

Still, the bad publicity for Ponzi was not yet over! On August 11, 1920, the front page of the newspaper headlined, "CANADIAN "PONSI" SERVED JAIL TERM." This article reported that Ponzi was sent to jail in Canada for forgery involving an Italian bank. The article revealed that Ponzi, Canadian Ponsi, was also known as Charles Bianchi. In Montreal, Ponzi, Bianchi, was remembered by one businessman who had dealings with him as "Bianchi, the snake!"

While somewhat short on facts and based mainly on interviews with people who knew Ponzi as a banker in Canada, the picture emerges of a shady operator who promised larger than normal returns to the poor Italian immigrants in Montreal. One person interviewed said of Ponzi, " Ponzi! Yes. In Boston he makes money and you praise him. Remember him? I remember him, and I remember Zarrossi…(owner of the bank) and all the dogs, well do I remember." He adds, "Ponzi, great Ponzi, what I tell you is Bianchi, crooked Bianchi and the great talks of bringing your money up to the skies that he told poor people. And their money, where did it go? In to pockets. I tell you, and I know it too."

Another Canadian called Ponzi, "a sporty feller." "He never liked to work…and was always talking of millions and wearing a nice white collar and nice clothes."

When contacted by *The Post*, Ponzi, of course, denied ever having been arrested for forgery. Regardless, the newspaper reported, and accurately so, that the net around Ponzi was drawing closer.

The Post reported that during the course of its investigation, contact with the postal authorities revealed there had been no large purchases of international postal reply coupons. In fact, there had never been enough coupons printed to meet the demand for coupons that Ponzi would have had to buy and redeem for his scheme work.

Once again, the SEC was swarmed by hundreds of promissory note investors wanting their money back. Ponzi, always nonchalant, served coffee and doughnuts and with a smile – gave back money. However, the gig was almost up.

The Securities Exchange Company Shuts Down

On August 12, 1920, Ponzi met with government officials and was formally informed that he and the SEC were, in fact, insolvent. While the exact amount of his insolvency has never been determined, it is estimated that Ponzi showed a deficit between $5 and $10 million. It was learned that Ponzi may have purchased no more than a handful of postal coupons during the eight or nine months he was operating. He was simply paying investors back with their own money or with money received from other investors. He was subsequently arrested on 86 counts of mail fraud and the Hanover Trust Bank was closed. He plead guilty to using the mails to defraud and was sentenced to five years in federal prison. After serving about 3 ½ years he was released from federal prison and shipped back to the state of Massachusetts where he faced theft charges for his involvement in the investment scheme. Ponzi was again convicted after a speedy trial and this time sentenced to serve seven to nine years in state prison. Ponzi posted an appeal bond and made his way to Florida to make a comeback.

While in Florida he became involved in a land fraud scheme in Duval County. He was indicted by a Duval County grand jury and after a short jury trial was convicted for violations of Florida's statutes regulating operations under a 'Declaration of Trust.' He received a one-year prison sentence for that crime. Eventually, Ponzi returned to Massachusetts where he served out his original seven to nine year prison term. He was paroled in 1934, some 14 years after the start of his SEC operation. He was then quickly deported back to Italy.

Quite famous by now, Ponzi became associated with the Italian dictator Benito Mussolini. Mussolini gave Ponzi a job in the financial section of his government, but that job didn't last long. While in Italy,

Ponzi continued to scheme. He came up with the idea of selling shares in his autobiography to investors. Ponzi figured that he could sell 1,000 shares in his book and that he could sell the book for $25.00 thereby earning about $25 thousand. Unfortunately, no one was interested.

Ponzi eventually wound up in Rio de Janeiro, Brazil, where he died on a charity ward in 1949. It has been said that the only thing Ponzi left behind on the nightstand by his deathbed was – his autobiography. A copy of which you now hold in your hands. The book was privately published in the past, but never in large quantities. In fact, copies of that earlier edition are quite rare. His autobiography is now part of the public domain.

This is, to the best of my knowledge, the first time Ponzi's book has been professionally published for a large reading audience. I hope you enjoy his story as much as I did.

Sincerely,

Mark Mathosian, Editor/Publisher
Naples, Florida
July 15, 2001

INTRODUCTION

MEET MR. PONZI, THE CHAMPION GET-RICH-QUICK WALLINGFORD OF AMERICA

"Ponzi is the guy who put the crease in Croesus," wrote Neal O'Hara for the Boston Traveler toward the end of July, 1920. "He is the guy that ran up millions from a two cent stamp. If five-spots were snow flakes, Ponzi would be a three day blizzard."

"You've got to hand it to his credit. He makes your money gain 50 percent in 45 days, which is as much as the landlords do. He delivers the goods with postage stamps, which is more than Burleson does. The way Ponzi juggles the reds and the greens, he makes Post Office look like a child's game. He simply buys stamps in Europe while the rest of the boys are buying souvenir post cards. And a postage stamp is still worth two cents in spite of the service you get for it, and any yap knows that you cannot get stuck on postage stamps unless you sit on the gluey side up!"

"Ponzi's way is cheaper than making money with your own sextuple press. The way he's got it fixed with postage stamps, the Government does the printing for him. He stretches a dollar into a million with all his sleeves rolled up. You furnish the dollar and Ponzi tosses in the six zeros in back of it. This baby can turn decimal points into commas on almost any bank-book. The way that Ponzi has money here and in Europe goes to prove that half of the world are squirrels and the other half nuts. The only thing that's got 'em worried is that they don't know which side is furnishing the nuts."

"Worried" isn't the half of it. According to Miss Marguerite Mooers Marshall, a staff writer for the New York Evening World, Ponzi had them in a frenzy. Listen to what she said:

"Whoever said that proud old New Englanders are conservative, undoubtedly made that statement before the advent of Charles Ponzi. Today all Boston is get-rich-quick mad over him, the creator of fortunes, the modern King Midas who doubles your money in ninety days. Did I say Boston? My mistake. I should have said the entire New England, from Calais, Maine, to Lake Champlain, from the Canadian border to New Jersey."

"At every corner, on the street-cars, behind the department store counters, from luxurious parlors to humble kitchens, to the very outskirts of New England, Ponzi is making more hope, more anxiety, than any conquering general of old. Mary Pickford, Sir Thomas Lipton and smuggling booze over the Canadian border aren't in it any more."

"For Ponzi makes everybody rich quick. Loan him your money, from fifty dollars to fifty thousand dollars, and in 180 days he gives you back twice as much as you gave him. He has been doing it for eight months and he is still at it."

"With no other security than his personal note, Boston is pouring all its savings into Ponzi's hands. Like a tidal wave the passion for investment with the now Italian banker has swept over Boston folk until it took half of the Boston's police force to subdue the enthusiasm of a throng of prospective investors overflowing from the banking office, through the corridors, down the stairs, and into the street, blocking the traffic."

In the opinion of Miss Marshall, "Ponzi belongs to America, the land of 520 per cent Miller, of the man who cornered wheat, of all the other get-rich-quick Wallingfords!"

Regardless of what may develop as to the "righteousness and legality of the methods by which Ponzi, according to his own admission, has cleaned up in six months a fortune for himself, has given thousands of investors 50 per cent on their money, has operated from a central office of two rooms attended by twelve clerks and has done the whole blessed thing with postage stamps-nothing in the world but postage stamps, plus a knowledge of the world postage regulations and of foreign exchange, plus an idea of magnificent simplicity and apparently bombproof consistency, plus all the nerve there is to it," she thought the world would agree with her that Ponzi. "would be wasted anywhere else than in America."

"Ponzi stands as the premier get-rich-quick financier of the age," conceded the Washington Post.

When, according to the Rochester Times-Union, "a man untaught in finance shows Wall Street and the greatest financiers in the world that they are pikers, whether the Ponzi bubble bursts or not, the American people will take off their hats to a fellow so clever as he," because as Arthur B. Reeve explained it, although Ponzi might be "a product of conditions… his success is nevertheless the result of his own remarkable personality. Not every one can step out on a street corner and persuade the passersby by the thousands to give him their pay envelopes - even on a chance of a return as great as 400 per cent a year." And the Washington Evening Star agreed that "whether he retires as a millionaire or is finally detected as a swindler, Ponzi must stand as a remarkable figure" and "it must be said of him that whatever his game, he has certainly played it well."

CHAPTER I

MR. PONZI LANDS IN BOSTON WITH $2.50 TO ADD A $15,000,000.00 CHAPTER TO THE HISTORY OF STATE STREET FINANCE.

November 15, 1903, was a Sunday. A fall day typical of the New England shores, with a fine, steady drizzle blown in by an icy East wind over miles and miles of ocean. One of those exasperating days on which only the sacred cod-fish of Massachusetts would defy the elements along Tremont Street and around the Boston Common without a diving suit on.

In the harbor and on the water front, the drizzle and the East wind were even more intense. From the expanse of the Atlantic, they seemed to converge upon a point between Castle and Governor's Island and blow with added force along the path of the narrow ship channel, beating up thousands of whitecaps from a dirty and murky looking sea surface.

On that Sunday morning the S. S. Vancouver of the Old Dominion Line could be seen coming up the Boston harbor shortly after 8 o'clock. She was progressing slowly and majestically, pitching occasionally where the channel was deeper and rougher. In those days, a ten-thousand-ton vessel was no fishing boat and the Vancouver was well justified to feel as self-conscious of her size as a modern Cunarder.

A little ways up the harbor, the ship pulled up alongside the Company's pier in East Boston. The gang planks were lowered. A motley crowd of passengers who had been lining the decks began to ooze out of her side and onto the dock.

They were immigrants. Immigrants of various nationalities, but predominantly Italians. Most of them had traveled in steerage, some in first or second class. But they were all immigrants. They were all men, women or children who had left their native country and come to America, temporarily or for good, with the common purpose of finding better wages, better living conditions and greater economic independence.

I was one of those immigrants; one of the motley crowd oozing out of the ship's side; a diminutive figure bedecked in expensive clothes of the latest European cut and followed down the gang-plank by a couple of stewards laden with several pieces of baggage, large and small, labeled "First Class."

Truly, for an immigrant, I did not look the part. There was nothing in my appearance to suggest the breadwinner; nothing that could be even remotely associated with the thought of manual labor, of work of any kind; of economic penury. From tie to spats, I looked like a million dollars just out of the mint; like a young gentleman of leisure, perhaps like the scion of wealthy parents on a pleasure tour. And that goes to show that appearances don't mean a thing. In fact, I was in a jam right then and there-in an economic jam and a critical predicament at that and five thousand miles away from home and five hundred or more miles away from my ultimate destination, in a strange country, with no friends and no money. That's it. Broke right from the start, my entire resources in cash amounting to $2.50.

Less than two weeks before I had left Italy with $200, a maternal blessing and a buoyant frame of mind, bound for the United States. I had sailed on a definite mission and with a definite purpose; on a cinch, to get rich.

"Go and make a fortune and then come back," - had urged my elders - just like that and just as if amassing a fortune in America was something which could not be helped. "You can't miss it," - they had insisted to overcome my hesitancy. "In the United States the streets are actually strewn with gold; all you have to do is to stoop and pick it up." The events of later years showed that there was more truth than poetry in my elder's forecast. In fact, it has been my experience that I did not even have to stoop down to pick up the gold. In 1920 it was actually tossed into my lap; not by the pennyweight and with a teaspoon, but in large lumps and with a steam shovel.

Nevertheless, right after landing, as I was standing on the company's dock, on American soil, my predicament was much too critical. I still had the maternal blessing with which I had set sail but that was all. The $200 had dwindled down to $2.50 on the way over and a card sharp had taken me for most of it and the tips and the bar the rest of it. My buoyant frame of mind was buoyant no longer - it was top heavy. In fact, I stood there with my elders' assurances still ringing in my ears, ready to pick up the gold, but forced into the realization that I had been grossly duped. There was no gold at my feet or yellow nuggets strewn about; only mud - plain mud, sticky, black mud an inch deep which extended from the landing to the gate and beyond it away up the street as far as the naked eye could see. Just mud. And I had come all the way from Italy, over five thousand nautical miles of deep, blue water, to find nothing but mud and shattered dreams of untold wealth easily acquired.

The reason why Boston did not see much more of me at that time, on that particular occasion, must not be ascribed to snobbery on my part. It was that my destination had been planned in advance back home and the change had not been made on my part. I had been destined for Pittsburgh, the "Smoky City" of Pennsylvania, as the presumptive abode of some fifth cousin of some third cousin of ours. Allegedly, he was a railroad contractor, but in reality one not beyond petty pilfering during the slack season in grand larceny. Which goes to show that allegations in general, whether in court or elsewhere, must be, taken with a grain of salt.

Not only had my destination been planned ahead, but my elders had seen to it that their plans did not miscarry and I had been provided with unalienable wherewithals to get there. Wise old birds, my elders. They had a hunch, based upon experience that I might run out of cash before I got on the other side of the ocean, as I had been stranded before on much shorter trips. So they had furnished me with a prepaid railroad fare to Pittsburgh by way of New York. If they hadn't, Boston and I would have got acquainted that very same drizzling Sunday.

As it was, I did not leave the dock and with the rest of the New York bound immigrants. I waited on that pier until a special train picked as up about 9 P.M., and twelve solid hours in the cold, in the mud and without a thing to eat.

There is no doubt about that train being a special, I hope to tell it was. It was so far out of the ordinary for discomfort and everything else as to make a war-time 40 and 8 look like a Pullman in comparison. It was routed to New York over the Southern Pacific or the Santa Fe. It must have been, as nothing else could explain its getting into the Grand Central the day after at noon, unless it ran around in circles all night, or stopped at every crossing, or bowed at every telegraph pole. The well known slow train through Kansas was a streak of lightning alongside of ours.

When we reached New York I was on the verge of cannibalism. An early edition of Wimpy as my stomach had been idle so long that it had withered and I would have traded my soul for anything that I could sink my teeth into, be it a steak of the leather variety or a pole cat. So, the moment the brakes began to screech under the shed, I took a dive out of that train and made a bee-line for the gate.

The cop on duty did not like the idea of my making a race track out of the train shed and he spread out his arms and caught me on the fly. Notwithstanding his embrace, I knew that he was no lost brother of mine and resented his untimely affection. We exchanged words and many of them, but I could no more understand his Irish twang than he could my Italian. It was a draw, an impasse, rather, so we called in a bootblack to arbitrate. The situation cleared up immediately. The cop was told that I was hungry, starved and that I wanted to eat first and talk afterwards. He conceded that my haste, once explained, was beyond argument and withdrew and the bootblack and I withdrew in the direction of the nearest restaurant. We ate; that is, I presume that he did as I was too busy with my own meal to pay any attention to his. He paid the check, but ordinarily I would have paid it, and $2.50 did not permit me to stand on ceremonies, so I let him have his way and wince. After that one experience, I believe that bootblack lost all inclination to be hospitable to incoming immigrants. One such experience is enough for anybody. My appetite must have set him back the price of a suit of clothes with two pair of pants.

My next problem was to locate the Pennsylvania Station, which, at that time, had not moved into New York, but was still across the River, but I didn't know that, of course. All that I knew was that I had to go by street-car in one direction, then transfer to another car going in a different direction, then walk a couple of blocks to the right, then-Oh, what's the use. The gist of the thing is that I had to get there and did not have the slightest idea as to where or how. Old Teddy Roosevelt must have felt the same way when he was trying to trace the course of the River of Doubt in the Brazilian jungle.

The Pennsylvania Station proved to be the most elusive thing I ever chased after in all my life, girls included. Whenever I inquired about it, it seemed to be just around the corner -like Mr. Hoover's prosperity. But I rounded dozens of corners and walked dozens of miles and blocks in all directions before I could establish even a remote contact with it. Eventually, I got there, yes, after I discovered that I must head for a ferry boat in order to land on the New Jersey side of the River. But I got there exhausted - numb-dead. For the best part of an afternoon I had been going around loaded with "light" baggage, so-called. Light, from the stand point of size and space, but not of weight, because it felt like lead. And when the Pennsylvania Station hove in sight, I wasn't interested in trains any longer and I didn't give a hoot whether I got to Pittsburgh or not, or whether I never hobnobbed with the Carnegies, the Fricks and the Mellons. All I craved for was a coffin; a yielding, comfortable one in which I could lay my aching limbs for an eternal rest.

CHAPTER II

MR. PONZI BOBS UP IN MONTREAL WITH ONE DOLLAR AND BUYS HIMSELF A PECK OF TROUBLE.

To have landed in America without money was not half as bad as having landed without the least knowledge of its language. I could not fill an office job because I did not speak or understand a word of English. What I knew of other languages did not help. Likewise, my general education was useless. As a student and a man of frail physique, I was not cut out for manual labor. Still, I had to live. And in order to earn a living I had to work at something.

During the four uneventful years which followed my arrival into the United States, I filled a number of menial jobs. Jobs that I detested and loathed. Jobs at which I was invariably underpaid for my needs and overpaid for what I deserved. I filled them as a matter of necessity. Not of choice. And the net result was that I did not make any headway. I lived and that is all. But to live is to learn. And I learned. Every day served to add a few words to my English vocabulary.

I tried my hand at everything. From grocery clerk to road drummer. From sewing machine repair man to insurance salesman. From factory hand to kitchen and dining room help. In some of the jobs I lasted no time. In others, I lasted longer. Often, I would be fired. Oftener, I would quit of my own accord either disgusted or to avoid being fired. I shifted from one city to another. Sometimes by rail. Others, by foot. Pittsburgh, New York, Paterson, New Haven, Providence, and then ... Montreal, Canada.

I don't know what brought me up there. The summer heat, maybe. Or fate. But one afternoon of July 1907, I alighted at the Gare Bonaventure with no baggage and a dollar bill in my pocket. Now a dollar isn't much at any time. On or off the gold standard. In a strange country, it was still less. It was, however, a sufficient incentive for me to get busy and do something.

I got busy. Within two blocks of the railroad station, up St. James Street, I spied the sign of the Banco Zarossi and went right in. In less than five minutes I was signed up as a clerk. The first congenial job I had struck in four years!

Louis Zarossi and I got along fine. He was a big hearted man, good natured, liberal, jolly and, I dare say, on the level. Much more on the level than many I have met since, although coated with a veneer of respectability. While it is true that later events gave Zarossi a sort of a black eye, it is my opinion - my expert opinion of him - that he was the victim of circumstances and bad associations rather than a man of evil intent and dishonest inclinations.

Around that time, Zarossi was well fixed. His Italian bank was doing a land office business. His reputation and credit were of the best. But he was easily led.

The usual run of dimeless promoters and sponges began to buzz and flock around him. The successful man is never without them, if he is easy with them. They can smell a sucker further and quicker than a buzzard can a corpse. They got him to engage in a number of activities. The new enterprises needed money. And he began to dip into his depositors' accounts; the same old story of a lot of bank executives. Some do it less skillfully than others and get caught. Some get away with it because they are either smarter or have more political pull.

To make a long story short, the time came when Zarossi found himself financially embarrassed. I enjoyed his full confidence and he told me of his predicament. He was not insolvent by any means. But some of his enterprises had not proved very productive and he needed some cash. Some new blood, so to speak.

Around that time who should show up in Montreal, but an old schoolmate of mine. He had come to Canada looking for business opportunities. We met, celebrated and talked. I explained to him Zarossi's situation. Brought the two together. And they made a deal. My old schoolmate sailed for Italy and returned in a few weeks with the money necessary to establish him in partnership with Zarossi.

Everything went along fine for a while. Things hummed. Then ...

came the revolution! Some of Zarossi enterprises went under. The rumor got around that he was in difficulties. The banks shut down his credit. His depositors began to withdraw their money.

There wasn't much that could be done to avert a disaster. But what had to be done, had to be done quick. Self preservation being the first law of nature, each party in interest thought of himself first and . . . the devil take the rest. Like some of the recent marine disasters. I had nothing to lose one way or the other. Except my job. So, I merely stood by, in the role of spectator, but I did not miss a thing of what was going on.

An emergency council was called into executive session to devise ways and means to keep Zarossi afloat. The council was made up of Zarossi, my old schoolmate and another man known as Spagnoli. That was not his real name. It was an alias. We knew not his real name. The police of his native city undoubtedly did. Hence the alias. Being in the confidence of all, I, of course, was the unavoidable fixture in the council room.

This old schoolmate was a peculiar sort of a fellow. Although illiterate, he had managed to amass quite a bit of money. Tainted money, it's true. But money nevertheless. If all that was said of him was true, he should have spent the best part of his life in jail. He probably ended there after I lost track of him, I don't know and I don't care.

In some way he had succeeded in winning Zarossi's confidence. It didn't take much to do that. Zarossi was always ready to welcome even a rattlesnake with open arm. Or, maybe, he had loaned Zarossi some money now and then. The fact is that "wherever Zarossi went, he was sure to go." Like Mary's little lamb.

At the emergency council's meeting, the old schoolmate got right down to brass tacks.

"Louis," he told Zarossi, "you must leave Canada. If you hang around another week, they will put you in jail for embezzlement and you'll never get out"

"But I can't run away" Zarossi protested, "I can't leave my family. I can't give up a business that I have built up so painstakingly!"

"Don't be a fool, Louis! He insisted. "This is no time to get sentimental. In jail you would not be any good to your family."

"But the situation is not desperate," interposed Zarossi. "I don't need much money to see me through."

"Little or much, it is more money than you can raise just now," retorted he.

"How so?" asked Zarossi in surprise. "You have told me that you would loan me the money, haven't you?"

"Have I? I don't remember," he replied. "At any rate, I couldn't give you a dime just now. My money is all tied up. I don't see any other way out for you, but to go."

Zarossi, deprived of financial assistance at the last minute, had to give in. He agreed to run away. He made a deal by which my old schoolmate was to appear as his major creditor, petition him in bankruptcy after he had left, then offer to settle with the other creditors at two cents on the dollar. Through that deal he hoped to get hold of Zarossi's assets which, if properly administered and liquidated, would have paid much more than 2%, and benefit thereby at the creditor's expense.

"You go along and don't worry," he told Zarossi. "As soon as I have possession of your assets, I will go 50-50 with you." And Zarossi believed him. But he was planning all the time to cheat him too.

In fact, a day or two later, while the three of us were having a drink in a barroom up St James Street, he asked Zarossi to give him a forged note.

"Make out a note to me for a small sum and sign So-and So's name to it," he said to him.

"But that would be forgery," protested Zarossi.

"Sure. I want it to be forgery," he admitted. "I want to make sure you will not come back to Canada, under some promise of immunity, before I lay my hands on your assets. I've got to protect myself. I'll keep the note, but will not use it against you except in the event you should come back of your own accord and spoil my plans."

Zarossi did as he was told. He gave him the note. I don't remember any more what name he did sign to it. Nor the amount. A few days later, he left Canada and went to Mexico. But before he left, he assigned to my old schoolmate some negotiable property which the bank owned out West. Enough to reimburse him for his investment. To me he assigned ... the care of his family. Wife and three kids. Or were they four? I don't remember. But they were more than I had bargained for.

CHAPTER III

MR. PONZI FALLS FROM THE FRYING-PAN INTO THE FIRE AND WONDERS WHAT IT IS ALL ABOUT

At the beginning, there was an awful fuss over Zarossi's flight. Some of the depositors were real ugly. They made things generally unpleasant all around. They threatened Zarossi's family. Even my own life. But things cooled down after a while. They always do. If they didn't, there would be more bank executives hanging from tree limbs, than running around in Rolls Royces or smoking dollar cigars behind mahogany desks. And that, - God forbid! - would be one form of bank insurance that would bring home the bacon without "ifs" and "buts."

The Zarossi family left their pretentious apartment and moved with me into a couple of furnished rooms. We shared with the landlady the use of the kitchen, bath, parlor and dining-room. I went to work. Yes, on the stagger plan; now and then. The two oldest girls went to work too. The mother remained home to cook the meals and mind the house.

We led a very modest and retired life. Entirely too much so. Hardly went anywhere. We spent our evenings at home yawning until bed time. But that could not last long. I was then 26 and very susceptible to girlish charms. Zarossi's eldest daughter was 17 and very pretty. The inevitable happened. We fell in love with each other. And yawned no longer evenings.

My old schoolmate was a frequent visitor at the house. He was about my age, and equally susceptible to a girl's charms, and he fell in love too, with the same girl. But I had the edge on him. His love never got to first base.

In so far as I was concerned, his being in love with my girl did not affect my friendship for him. For the very good reason that I did not know he was in love. I learned of it later. Too late, in fact, to put me on my guard. In so far as he was concerned, I am inclined to believe that his disappointment drove him actually insane. No sane person would have done to me what he did, unless he was the reincarnation of perfidy.

It happened in the summer of 1908. For some time he had been telling me that he intended to go out West to liquidate his interests in the independent branches of the Banco Zarossi. There were three of those branches. One in Sudbury, Ontario; one in Calgary, Alberta; and one in Fernie, British Columbia. I had established them and knew all about them.

He hesitated going because he was neither familiar with the language, nor the country, nor the business. He suggested that I go first and he would follow me. I told him I had no money to undertake such trip. He said he would furnish the money and allow me a commission, and I agreed to go.

One Saturday we met in St. James Street by prearrangement. We went into the Bank of Hochelaga, in which he had an account, and he presented a check for certification. It was the closing hour or a few minutes after. I remember that, because the time had something to do with his alleged inability to cash the check right there and then. But I do not vouch for either the veracity or the accuracy of the allegation.

His failure to cash the check seemed to preclude my departure which had been set for the coming Monday. I could not go away for a month or two, on such a long trip, without a trunk, some clothes and a few things. All purchases which I had planned to make that same Saturday afternoon. But he said that he might be able to cash the check elsewhere.

In the evening, when he came over to the house, he still had the check. He hadn't been able to do anything with it.

"There is a chance," he said, "that they might cash it at one of the Hochelaga branches which are open Saturday evenings. What do you say? Shall we try?"

I agreed that we should. So, we left the house and went to the branch in St. Catherine Street. He walked up to the paying-teller's window, exchanged a few words and got the cash. About $400.

We left the bank, made some purchases and went home to pack. All

I had of mine did not fill one half of the trunk.

"Tomorrow I will bring some of my stuff to fill the trunk," said he and left.

The next day he came over and brought what he wanted me to take along. Mostly papers in large envelopes. He gave me about $200 in cash, saying that he would buy me the ticket in the morning and bring it over.

Monday forenoon, I went out to buy a few more things. I came home about 11:30. As I stepped into the doorway, two plain clothes men put me under arrest and rushed me upstairs to my room. They frisked me and found the $200. They went through the trunk, discovered a number of blank checks among his papers, seized everything, and took me to headquarters. There, I found myself locked up on a charge of forgery and held incommunicando.

I was dazed. I did not know what to think. I couldn't make head or tail of the whole thing. To make matters worse, I couldn't see anybody or talk with anybody.

From headquarters I was transferred later to the jail. While there, I was permitted to write letters. But I never received an answer to any of them. Never received a visit. Never saw a newspaper. I was virtually buried alive and knew not what was going on outside.

Conditions in the jail beggar description. The place was filthy and infested with vermin. The moment they assigned me to a cell, I knew I could not stand it for twenty-four hours. So, I mustered up my wits to the rescue. I cuddled up in a corner of the bed, against the wall, with a vacant stare, chewing a towel to shreds. Other inmates, going by, observed me and reported to the guard. He came over and had me transferred to the jail hospital.

There, I threw a couple of war whoops and started to climb a barred window. Two orderlies took hold of me and put me into a straight jacket. I lay still for a couple of hours. Then I acted as if I was coming to from an epileptic attack. The straight jacket was removed and I was given a bed and a milk diet. Bread and milk were the only things fit to eat in that jail. The ruse enabled me to remain in the hospital all the time I was in jail. Conditions there were far from pleasant, but bearable.

One day, probably a mouth or so later, I learned, through the usual prison channels, that Zarossi was also a guest in the same jail. He had arrived the night before, brought back from Mexico under extradition proceedings. I asked to see him and was allowed.

My old schoolmate had doublecrossed him. Unable to effect a compromise with the other creditors and get hold of Zarossi's assets, he blamed him for it. He had tried to blackmail him and his wife without success. So, he had turned right round and demanded Zarossi's extradition on the strength of the forged, note.

Zarossi and I put our heads together and went over the situation. We found that only my testimony could convict him. As that of my old schoolmate could not do it. But, being in jail, I could not flee the jurisdiction of the court. Therefore, it was up to me to decide what to do. Whether to side with a despicable crook like my old schoolmate, or with Zarossi, a friend and my girl's father beside. I could not hesitate. I did not hesitate. I decided to save Zarossi, cost what it may.

A few days later, his case came up for a hearing. I was summoned as a witness. My old schoolmate took the stand first and accused Zarossi of having forged the note. After him, I was called to the stand to testify. I answered the preliminary questions. Then I was shown the forged note.

"Have you ever seen this note before?" I was asked.

"Yes, sir. I have." I answered.

"On what occasion did you see it?" was the next question. I related the circumstances under which I had seen it. In a barroom in St. James Street.

"Who was present on that occasion?" inquired the Crown prosecutor.

I mentioned my old schoolmate and myself.

"Was anyone else there?" insisted the prosecutor.

"No, sir. Only the two of us," I stated.

"Wasn't Zarossi there too?" asked the prosecutor a little provoked, because I was supposed to be his witness.

"No, sir. Zarossi was not there," I maintained.

The prosecutor shifted the attack from another angle.

"Do you know who wrote that note?" he asked point blank

"I do," I replied calmly.

"Who wrote it?" he continued, believing he had me in a corner.

"I did," I replied.

"You did? You wrote that note?" exploded the Prosecutor - at my unexpected answer.

"Yes, air. I did," I confirmed with the same nonchalance of a George Washington under the cherry tree.

"All of it," I said.

The hearing ended right there and then. My old schoolmate left the courtroom in a rage: like a wild man. The prosecutor asked the court to dismiss the charge. The judge ordered Zarossi discharged, but gave him twenty-four hours to leave Canada. I went back to the jail.

Before I left the courtroom, the prosecutor, a young Italian, came up to me.

"You lied and you know you did!" he whispered to me in our native language.

"Of course, I did. But you can't prove it," I replied to him with a grin.

"I don't hold it against you, Charlie," he said then. "Zarossi is a darned sight better man than the complainant."

Back in the jail, there was nothing else for me to do than to await patiently my own trial. Zarossi had left Montreal, followed shortly afterwards by his family. Their destination, was unknown. My old schoolmate apparently, had also dropped out of sight.

I was brought into court in October, I believe. There for the first time, I learned the exact nature of the charges against me. I was accused of having forged that very check which my old schoolmate had presented for certification and payment. I don't remember whose name had been forged. That of some shipping broker, I believe. And the amount was around $400.

I pleaded not guilty. The witnesses were called to the stand to testify. Four of them, I think. The man whose name had been forged, the two detectives and the paying teller. The shipping broker said he knew me. Said I had called at his office occasionally on Zarossi's business. That, was true. He also stated that the check had been torn from the back of his check book. Undoubtedly, that was also so. But he was unable to say whether I had done it. He had not seen me around his office about that time.

The Rise Of Mr. Ponzi

The two detectives testified to have found a number of blank checks in my trunk and $200 in my pocket.

"What has become of that money inquired the judge." "Is it here?"

"No, your Honor," answered one of the detectives. "It has been returned to the bank."

"Returned to the bank?" asked the judge rather amazed. "And upon whose authority?"

"It was the bank's money," explained the witness. "We saw no reason for holding it."

"That's it," interrupted the judge, considerably provoked. "The police take it upon themselves to decide what is and what is not material evidence. If it had been some poor man's money he would have not got it back so easily. But, being the money of the Bank of Hochelaga, a great bank, the police must go out of their way, actually violate the law, to see to it that the bank is not inconvenienced."

"I am going to adjourn this case and look into the matter. I want to see where the responsibility rests for the unwarranted return of that money. Upon the proper identification of that money, hinges, to a large extent, the defendant's guilt or innocence. He has a right to be confronted with the alleged proofs against him. He has a legitimate title to that money until it has been properly identified in this court as someone elses property."

After that blasting from the bench, a blasting which made headlines in the Montreal papers, I went back to the jail in high spirits, I felt reasonably sure that the judge would dismiss the case. And that goes to show how little I knew judges at that time.

In fact, when the trial was resumed, the judge's attitude was changed. The money incident was dropped. The last witness was called to the stand. He was the paying-teller.

"Is this the man who presented the check and to whom it was paid?" the prosecutor asked him pointing to me.

The paying-teller said he "presumed" I was the man. Three months had elapsed and he had not seen me since, he admitted. However, he was under the impression that the man who presented the check was taller, thinner, clean shaved and had light hair. His description certainly did not fit me. It was more like that of my old schoolmate.

For an identification, it was a corker! But it got by. Anything would have got by that day. Besides, I couldn't butt in because I was represented by counsel. I hadn't mentioned that. But I had a lawyer. He had volunteered to represent me gratis because I had saved his client from jail.

He was the least loquacious member of the bar I ever ran across. Cal Coolidge was actually garrulous alongside of that lawyer. Throughout the whole trial, he never cross-examined a witness, he never put in an objection, he never so much as glanced in my direction. The only thing he did was to get up, presumably to argue in my behalf, and say:

"If Your Honor please, I recommend my client to the mercy of this Court."

When I heard that, they could have knocked me down with a feather. He had virtually conceded my guilt even before the court had pronounced me guilty. In a way, I am glad he did not say any more. If he had, they would have hung me!

I got my first taste of legal uncertainties when the judge spoke:

"Notwithstanding the brilliant argument of counsel for the defense," he said, "the evidence compels me to find the defendant guilty of forgery as charged, etc…"

Now, can you tie that? Brilliant argument of counsel, etc…! He could have said just as well: "Failure of counsel to put up a defense, compels me to conclude that my belief in the defendant's guilt is shared by counsel . . ." and let it go at that. It wouldn't have been half as raw as the other way.

A few days later, the court sentenced me to three years of imprisonment in the St. Vincent de Paul Penitentiary. The same afternoon, I was transferred there from the jail. An hour afterwards, my own mother would not have recognized me. I was bathed, shaved, clipped, dressed in a hideous uniform, mugged, fingerprinted and numbered. I had ceased to be a citizen. To have a name of my own. I had become a number!

CHAPTER IV

BY ADDING TWO AND TWO TOGETHER, MR. PONZI DEVELOPS AN ANALYTIC MIND AND ARRIVES AT THE INEVITABLE HOUR

The St. Vincent de Paul Penitentiary was no kindergarten. It was a prison where a man did time every minute of the day. It was a gaol. A replica of the Old Bailey. Of the Bastille. Of the Chateau d'If of Count of Monte Cristo fame.

From the sack of corn leaves and cobs which served as a mattress to the basement dungeons, that prison was indeed a place of penance and punishment. But, with all of that, I cannot say that I have ever witnessed an act of brutality or cruelty. The rules were strict. The utmost severity prevailed. But the prisoners were not abused unnecessarily nor exposed to inhumane treatment.

Favoritism was not practiced there. Each man stood on his own merits, be he a banker or a laborer, a native or a foreigner. Each had to start from the bottom of the ladder and work his way up with good behavior and industry. Outside influence did not get beyond the gate. But there were opportunities for advancement. There were jobs better than others. Privileges to be earned, and a man had to earn what he got.

My first assignment was to be a shed where they "made little ones out of big ones." Just that. I was supposed to pound lumps of rock into gravel with a mallet for seven or eight hours every day, and I did it.

In the two or three months I was in that shed, I figure I crushed enough rock to gravel the Yellowstone National Park. I got to be so proficient at it, that they must have blasted a couple of mountain ranges out in the Rockies to keep me going. After I started on that job, British Columbia never looked the same. Had they kept me at it a little longer,

I would have flattened that province down smoother than a pancake!

Eventually, my prowess received recognition and I was promoted to a clerkship in the blacksmith shop. From there I graduated into the Chief Engineers office. Then, out front with the Chief Clerk and in the Warden's office. I couldn't go any further up without stepping out of the gate.

As the Warden's clerk, I had the freedom of the prison. I could go anywhere within the walls, at any time, without being escorted by a guard. I was permitted to talk to other prisoners on official business. But, of course, a guard forty feet away could not tell whether my conversations with other prisoners were official or private. So, I conversed frequently. Especially with an ex-banker, because what I wanted to know in the worst way was how in the world I could have been arrested on a Monday morning for a forged check cashed only the preceding Saturday night.

In the first place, it did not seem likely that the forgery could have been discovered in that short period of time. Secondly, since my name did not appear on the check and I was unknown at the bank and at police headquarters, it looked like a physical impossibility that I could be connected with that check within less than forty-eight hours.

A Monsieur Lecoq or a Sherlock Holmes could not have traced that check to me in forty-eight hours. Even a sorcerer or a fortune teller could not have done that. For the very good reason that any person gifted with superhuman vision would, in any event, have gone to Pizzoccolo first. Then perhaps, he would have come to me. But it was absolutely inconceivable that two detectives, who could not see further than their nose, should, although in error, outclass a Lecoq, a Sherlock Holmes; and even a seer!

When I explained the circumstances to the ex-banker, he said it was as clear as daylight that somebody had tipped off both the bank and the police.

"You see," he told me, "that check was drawn upon the main office and cashed at a branch on Saturday night. It could not have gone from the branch to the main office much before 10 o'clock Monday morning. Checks are usually held in banks longer than that, two or three days, sometimes. At the main office they had no way of telling it was forged, since they had not detected the forgery at the time of the certification. The man whose name had been forged did not know and could not know. He would have known of it only at the end of the mouth when he got his statement from the bank. Or, he might have learned of it before if the forged check should have caused him to overdraw his account."

"Then it is your opinion that somebody tipped the bank off?" I asked him.

"Of course," he said.

"But I don't believe anybody knew about the check, except my old schoolmate and myself," I hazarded.

"Then it's clear that he tipped off the bank," he affirmed.

"Impossible!" I declared, as if appalled at the enormity of the thing, "I could not believe that of him. Beside, he could not put me in trouble and keep out himself."

"Is that so?" the banker said a bit cynically. "Figure it out for yourself then. You are in trouble and he is not."

"Yes, but that is so because I did not mention his name," I explained in his justification.

"That's it! He was probably figuring you wouldn't," he retorted.

"Why wouldn't I?" I asked.

"Because, even if it dawned upon you that he was at the bottom of the whole thing, you could not have cleared yourself by blaming him," replied the ex-banker. "The evidence is just as strong against you as it way have been against him. The both of you would have been convicted. "By the way," he asked, "where is he now?"

"I don't know," I answered.

"Have you seen him since? Has he written to you? Has he helped you in any way?" continued the ex-banker in his cross-examination of me.

"No," I admitted, gradually impressed by his logic.

"Then, for the love of Mike, wake up and begin to realize that you have been done for to a crisp!" the ex-banker exploded. "Get even with him! Write a letter to the bank and tell on him! They may help you to get out."

"Oh, I wouldn't do that" I said rejecting the suggestion. "If I have any bones to pick with him I will look him up. I'll catch up with him some day!"

Little did I realize then how difficult it is to track down a man who does not want to be found. In fact, all my inquiries about him never got further than the West Coast. I heard he bought some moving picture shows. That he was at it for a couple of years. Then, I lost track of him entirely.

The main reason probably was that he was not the only one in that territory at that time opening up moving picture shows. There were others doing the very same thing. Adolph Zukor too, I believe, was there. Some did well, some went under. Zukor, for instance, did exceedingly well. He organized or acquired the Paramount. But my old schoolmate dropped out of sight as if the earth had swallowed him. He is either dead or he has been so successful in altering his identity as to defy recognition. It's true that we have never met face to face since. One such meeting might make all the difference in the world.

What started me on his trail was a visit from my Montreal landlady. She called at the prison shortly after my conversation with the ex-banker. I was hungry for news. News of my girl. Of Zarossi. Of everybody I knew.

"Zarossi is somewhere in the United States," she told me. "I don't know where. I never heard from any of them."

"Not even from Angelina?" I asked. She was my girl.

No. And you? Have you heard from her?" she inquired.

"No," I had to admit with a certain reluctance. I hated to think she had dropped me so abruptly. "Did she believe me guilty?" I asked.

"I could not say. She never said much," my landlady replied. "Only once she remarked that my old schoolmate, perhaps, knew more about it than we thought."

"She did? What could have made her say that?" I said wondering.

"I don't know," she answered. "I guess she did not like him much because he had been bothering her."

"He had been bothering her?" I asked considerably surprised. "When was that? After I was arrested?"

"No, no. Before," said my landlady somewhat disappointed at my lack of perception. "What's the matter with you? Were you blind? Hadn't you noticed that he too was stuck on Angelina?"

"Of course not," I said. "It's all news to me."

"Oh, you men are all alike!" she declared almost chagrined at her discovery that I was as dumb as the rest. "When you are wrapped up in a girl, you men never see what's going on around her!"

"Maybe you are right," I admitted without the least abashment. "But tell me some more. What's become of him?"

"I don't know," she replied. "I never saw him after you were arrested. I heard he went West."

"Has he ever written?" I asked her.

"No," she said. "But I have talked with a man who had met him out there."

"What was he doing?" I kept asking.

"It seems that he liquidated the branches and then started in business for himself," she replied.

"What business? Where?" I inquired further.

"I don't know where. In several places. All over, I guess," she informed me. "I heard he was buying or putting up small moving picture houses all over the West Coast."

"Then he must be doing well," I said.

"They say he was," she agreed.

That visit gave me all of the information I needed to figure out what had happened to me. There could be no longer any doubt that he had framed me. With jealousy as the motive, he had planned and executed the crime. Then he had fastened it on to me and led the police to my door. And he was doing well while I was doing ... time!

Fortunately, there is an end to everything. Even to a prison term. And the end of mine was approaching. Not very fast, it's true. But approaching nevertheless. In fact, approaching faster than I thought because I was not counting the unexpected. On a ... Never mind. I was going to let the cat out of the bag beforehand.

Here is what happened. One day, the 13th of July, 1910, I was sitting at the typewriter in the Chief Clerk's office. The Warden came in with a paper in his hand.

"Charlie," he said handing it to me. "I want you to make me a copy of this right away."

"All right, Warden," I said taking the paper from him. I put a sheet in the typewriter, I laid the one to be copied in front of me, and I started to write. It was a printed communication from the Governor General's office. I had typed scores of similar communications before. They all began the same way. This one looked like a pardon.

I kept on typing mechanically until I got to the inmate's name. The Warden was standing in the back of my chair watching me. When I got to the name, I paused petrified. My eyes felt blurred. I rubbed them with the back of my hand and looked again at that name. It was there. Just as plain as day. There could not be any doubt about it. It was a name I had not heard in twenty or more months. It was my name!

The Warden chuckled and patted me on the shoulder.

"You have deserved it, Charlie," he said with a fatherly inflection in his voice. "It is not for me to judge whether or not you should have been sent here in the first place. But, for your sake, I am glad it's over. Run along now and get dressed so that you can make the afternoon train for Montreal."

He did not have to urge me twice. I flew inside and up to the tailor-shop. I took the first suit they gave me. Who cared whether it fitted or not? Who cared for appearances? All that mattered was freedom. And two hours later I was on the street, dressed somewhat grotesquely, with only five dollars in my pocket but happy. I was a free man once more!

CHAPTER V

UNCLE SAM, IN THE PERSON OF AN IMMIGRATION INSPECTOR, PLAYS A DIRTY TRICK ON MR. PONZI.

Back in Montreal the same evening, I stayed with friends. I couldn't go to the Windsor Hotel on five dollars. Hardly anywhere, in fact, because the money had to last me until I landed a job. But I couldn't stay in the street either. So, I accepted the hospitality which was tendered to me by those kind hearts, figuring that in a couple of days or so I would be able to find work.

However, I soon discovered that I was entirety too optimistic. A few calls among people, who knew me and who, ordinarily, could have used my services, brought to me the realization that I was up against it. I had a prison record! I was a jail bird! They could not hire me. They would not have me around.

I explained my predicament to one of my old schoolmates, who was running a bank there, a combination of labor and steamship agency. He and I had worked together some years before. He suggested that I leave Montreal and return to the United States.

"They won't know of your record there," he said, "and you can find a job much more easily."

"I would like to go" I told him, "but I have not enough money for the fare."

"Where would you want to go?" he asked.

"New York, I guess, if I can," I replied. "But any other place will do. Buffalo, Rochester, Syracuse, anywhere."

"Why don't you try some smaller places instead?" he urged, "Nearer the border. You might get a job as a time-keeper and interpreter in some camp."

A few days later, he told me that there were some such camps around Norwood and Ogdenburg, in New York State.

"The fare isn't much," he said. "How are you fixed for money?"

"I am not very flush," I answered. "But I have put in a day here and a day there at odd jobs."

"Then I would go, if I were you," he urged on. "You will probably strike somebody we know in those camps. We sent a lot of men down that way when we were with Zarossi."

That, decided me. Zarossi had placed thousands of laborers in that territory. Both with railroads and private contractors. Zarossi's men had built the Transcontinental. They were everywhere. With the C. P. R., with the Grand Trunk, with the B. & M. On both sides of the border. And I, as one of Zarossi's former clerks, was fairly well known among contractors and foremen.

In the morning of July 30, 1910, I left Montreal. My old schoolmate was at the depot when I bought my ticket. With him were five men. Apparently, they were going my way. They were Italians. Newly arrived immigrants, and he asked me to look after them.

Give them a hand, Charlie," he said. "Tell them when to get off. They have to change trains at Norwood." I believe he mentioned Norwood, or some such place like that.

The train was one of those locals that stopped at every shed along the road, for ten and fifteen minutes at a stretch. It hobbled on most of the morning in the direction of the border and made it about noon. At the last station on the Canadian side, it settled down for what looked like a regular siesta.

A United States immigration inspector came on board and went through the coaches, pausing here and there to interview each passenger. Eventually, he got to where the five Italians and myself were. He spoke to them first. They did not understand a word. So, he turned to me.

"Are these men with you?" the inspector asked me.

"Not exactly'" I said, "but they are going my way and I have been asked to help them out."

"Where are they going" he inquired.

"I don't know for sure," I stated. "Somewhere near Norwood, I think."

"What are they going there for?" he pressed on.

I had to ask the men before I could answer that question. They said they were going on some job. I believe they even exhibited some letter to show their destination.

"Where are they coming from?' the inspector wanted to know.

"From Montreal," I replied.

"All right," he said, and he walked along into the next coach.

Five minutes later, the train started off again. The next stop was Moers Junction, N.Y., on the United States side of the border. We were looking indifferently out of the window at the usual activity which follows the arrival of any train, when somebody yelled out:

"Hey, you men!"

We turned around and saw the immigration inspector on the doorway of the coach. He was addressing us. No doubt about that.

"You men get off this train and follow me," he directed. I conveyed his order to the five Italians and we did as were told. He took us to a little shack. A sort of an office. There he informed us that we were under arrest. He said we had violated the immigration laws of the United States.

The same afternoon, we were transferred to Rouses Point, N.Y., and locked up. A couple of days later, we were brought to Plattsburg and put in jail there to await trial in the Fall. I was held for smuggling aliens into the United States. The five Italians were held as material witnesses.

The whole thing did not seem to make sense. I tried to figure it out. But gave it up as a bad job. Finally, I had a chance to see an assistant United States Attorney. I told him the facts. He listened.

"You brought those men into the United States in violation of our immigration laws," he said.

"I did nothing of the kind" I retorted. "They came of their own accord. We were merely on the same train."

"But you've helped them. You have acted as interpreter for them," he insisted.

"Why shouldn't I have acted as interpreter?" I shot back at him. "It seems to we that I have helped both sides, in any case."

"At any rate," he continued. "You have all effected an illegal entry into the United States. None of you had a permit to enter."

"I, for one, did not know a permit was necessary," I explained. "Since I went to Canada three years ago, I have come in and out of the United States half a dozen times without a permit. I was never asked for one. I never met with an immigration inspector on the train. The only officials I ever ran across at the border were custom officers. They would come aboard and inspect the baggage."

"That does not alter the fact that this time you are all in the United States illegally," he went on.

"I won't concede even that," I told him. "We were interviewed on the Canadian side of the border. The train was not in motion. If we were not admissible for any reason, it seems to me that that was the time to exclude us. The inspector should have told us then."

"The inspector does not need to be told by you what he should or should not have done," the attorney interrupted.

"It seems to me that he does too," I poured back at him, losing my head. "It was his duty to warn us. To keep us from violating the law. Regardless of whether or not we were ignorant of the law. Instead, he actually coaxed us, led us, into a violation of the law in order to make a record for himself. I have no earthly use for that sort of public official. He, and not I, is the one who should be charged with smuggling those aliens."

"You will sing a different tune in a couple of months from now," he threatened with a leer.

"Maybe I will and, yet, maybe I won't," I snapped back. By then I was ready to relegate him to the seventh hell. If I didn't tell him so, he certainly read my mind because he brought the interview to a close.

All five of us languished in the Plattsburg jail until October. We could not raise bail. Fortunately, I had a cell all to myself, while other prisoners were required to bunk together. I managed to kill time sleeping and reading old magazines. But jail life, with its depressing idleness, began to get on my nerves. Two months of it had put me in a frame of mind where I no longer cared what happened to me, so long as I could have it over with.

Evidently, that assistant United States Attorney was a psychologist. I will let it go at that. It is not exactly what I thought he was, But "psychologist" sounds better. He knew or sensed that I was ripe for any sort of an approach. Just think of it! What an uncanny intuition that man had! He was utterly wasted in a district attorney's office! He was a naturally born "con" man! One who could tell and play a sucker better than any professional.

He sent for me. Told me how sorry he was about the whole thing. How he hated to go through with it. But his duty was clear. He was under oath to uphold and preserve the Constitution ... etc. It never occurred to me then to tell him that the Constitution had been preserved so long that it was actually pickled! Instead, I felt so blue ever his predicament that it almost brought tears to my eyes! It certainly was a darned shame that any scalliwag like me should be permitted to put such a nice man in that kind of stew!

The situation was so tense, that I actually expected him any minute to fall all over me and weep! I was scared. The prison suit I had on was not pre-shrunk. A good cry and it would have been all over with it. It would have left me looking like a bell-boy in shorts!

"Charlie," he said (they always call me Charlie when they want to stick me). "I want to help you. You are a pretty good sort of a fellow. Will you take my advice?"

"Sure," I told him before I knew what the advice was. "I'll do anything you say, bud . . ." I was about to say "buddy" but I corrected myself and changed it to "sir".

"Then plead guilty," he urged with an entreating look on his face.

"I will, like hell!" I jumped up. I might have felt softhearted. But not that soft.

"Don't get excited, Charlie," he purred on, "I am your friend. I am advising you for your own good. If you go through with the trial, you will be convicted. The evidence is against you. The judge will believe the inspector. He won't believe you, because you have a prison record. You would be licked before you started."

In that I agreed with him. I did not tell him so. But I knew even then how hopeless it was to buck the government without shekels or influential friends. However, I did not give in right away.

"If I am convicted, I won't be any worse off than if I plead guilty," I said.

"Oh, yes, you will," he rebutted. "The judge won't feel so inclined to be lenient. He might send you away for a long stretch. Make an example of you. The penalty is two years and $1,000 fine for each alien. In your case he would give you ten years and $5,000 fine."

"Not if I plead guilty, what will happen?" I asked.

"Not much, I guess," he said shrugging his shoulders. "Perhaps a $50 fine."

"But I can't pay the fine," I told him. "I haven't $50."

"In that case, you will have to serve a month in jail for it," he explained.

"Are you sure?" I insisted.

"Practically," he confirmed. "It is up to me to recommend the penalty. Judges always take the district attorney's recommendations."

"And you promise to let me off with a $50 fine if I plead guilty?" I asked him again.

"Yes," he said, "I promise you that I will speak to the judge."

And he did! But God, the judge and himself only know what he told him! I kept my end of the bargain. I pleaded guilty. Then he walked up to the bench. He handed some papers to the judge. He whispered to him. The judge glanced through the papers and took a squint at me. Then he said.

"Oh, what's the use ... Two years and $500 fine" and he passed the papers along to the clerk.

Somebody, a deputy-marshal, I guess, took me by the arm and led me out of the court room before I had time to realize what had happened. If he hadn't done that, I might have had to face additional charges of assault and battery and contempt, I was so mad, I was fit to be tied!

A couple of days later, I and four more federal prisoners, with a couple of deputy-marshals, started on our way South to serve our respective sentences in the United States Penitentiary at Atlanta, Ga.

The five Italians were discharged from custody right after my trial. They were paid their two or more months allowance as government witnesses. They were legally permitted to remain in the United States! Can you, reader, figure that out? I can't. I have been trying to ever since, but without success.

CHAPTER VI

MR. PONZI SWAPS A 2x4! COUNTY JAIL FOR UNCLE SAM'S $10,000,000 BIG-HOUSE.

On the way South, we traveled by Pullman, had our meals in the dining-car, and lounged about in our seats like tourists. In Washington, we had lunch at a pretentious restaurant near the station. Then we took a walk through the Capitol grounds. We would have gone inside, but were afraid to embarrass some of the boys.

We did not visit at the White House either. President Taft asked to be excused. He was busy. Probably figuring how he could beat Teddy Roosevelt at the next presidential elections. But figures do lie sometimes!

In Atlanta, the deputy-marshals took us to a "bar-room" (?!..) for a bracer. Something to pep us up before the ordeal of a prison commitment. The hardest stuff there, was near-beer! Flatter than a flat tire. It was nowhere "near" anything. In fact, it was so far from any beer taste that it could not have caught up with it in a coon's age. We drank it and groaned. Keeled over, almost!

We found the United States Penitentiary a sight for sore eyes. It wasn't anything like what we had seen before. Not I, at least. In those days, it had the reputation of being a Biltmore, a Ritz-Carlton in its line. And it lived up to its reputation too! Why wouldn't it? It was the potential abode of every big man in the country. "Big" from the standpoint of money, power or brains. From cabinet members and members of Congress to national bank officials and postal clerks. From income-tax dodgers to bootleggers and mail-robbers. And it stands to reason that those birds, knowing that an ounce of prevention is worth two pounds of cure, would take the New Willard as a pattern for "their" prison. They probably figured that, since it had to be a cage, it might as well be a gilded cage.

I didn't have much trouble down there in getting myself a clerical job. I found it waiting for me. In the laundry. But my knowledge of Italian, English and French got me promoted. I was transferred to the mail clerk's office, who by the way, is now the present Warden of that institution. Beside addressing and sealing envelopes, it was my duty to translate into English and type all incoming and outgoing mail, if written in any of the foreign languages with which I was more or less familiar. Particularly so, all correspondence from and for Ignazio Lupo and his alleged co-partners in crime.

Lupo was supposed to be an early edition of Al Capone. He was doing 30 years for counterfeiting. The same as Capone is doing eleven years for not having paid an income-tax. Actually; Lupo was doing time for all the crimes which were attributed to him. Among them, he was reputed to have ordered the killing in Sicily of Lieutenant Petrosino of the New York police force.

Far be it from me to uphold murder or any form of crime. I believe that a man ought to be punished for his misdeeds. But I believe also that he should be dealt with on the level. That he should be punished for what be has actually done. And not over punished, for a minor infraction or punished for something he never did, even if the man deserves ten times as much for other things which cannot be proved against him.

Of his other alleged crimes, I don't know anything about. I don't care and don't want to know. They are something between him and his Maker and no business of mine in any way, shape or form.

Lupo approached me in the prison yard during a ball game. He asked me whether I would mind moving into the same cell with him. He said that the prison officials, acting upon instructions were giving him one stool-pigeon after another for a cell-mate. Which was true. They were driving him crazy. He wanted somebody whom he knew wouldn't be there just to hurt him.

His plight was distressing. Regardless of the fact that a man with a 30-year sentence is not apt to prove a very cheerful companion, I told him I would ask to move in with him. We were put together. And I found much in him that I liked.

He was extremely good-hearted. Frank, direct and with "guts." After I got to know more about his case, I became convinced that he had been used to further the advancement of one of the officers of the United

States Secret Service. If I needed any evidence of it, I got it on my release from Atlanta. I had promised Lupo that I would call on the editors of the Atlanta Constitution and of the Atlanta Journal and give them the facts. I kept my promise. But the editors talked and the Secret Service got wind of it. One day, two of those guys cornered me in Peachtree Street and warned me to keep my nose out of Lupo's case.

"If you don't, inside of a week we will have you back with him for a long stretch," they threatened and they meant it too.

Evidence of Secret Service activities was not lacking even at the prison, anyway. An operator, Italian, had been attached to the mail clerk's office as an assistant. He wore a uniform and also did guard duty.

But his main function was to check my translations in general, and of Lupo's letters in particular, and forward copies to Washington. What the Secret Service were after, was evidence of Lupo's connection with other crimes. They assumed he would be fool enough to let the cat out of the bag someday, if there was any cat in the bag. And they never stopped to think that I was his cell-mate and helped him write those letters. Letters which I knew I would have to translate later for their benefit! Of all the dumb Alecs, they surely deserved the blue ribbon!

My job kept me out of the cell Sundays and holidays. Not to work. Just to sit around the office with other clerks. To smoke, talk or play checkers and chess. With us was Charles W. Morse, the same who had been rubbing elbows with the Big Wigs in Wall Street. The same to whom a well-known steamship company was said to have handed a cool million dollars on his release from prison.

Charlie Morse was a pretty good sort of a fellow. Loaded with money. Liberal. A good mixer. And extremely well versed in Wall Street finance. He could read the stock exchange quotations backwards.

One day he walked into Warden Moyer's office and asked him for the privilege to send a code wire to his brokers. The Warden, after much arguing back and forth, finally gave in. He told him not to make it a practice and send only that one wire along. Charlie did.

Several days later, again he walked into the Warden's office and handed him a check for $2,000 to bearer. The Warden wanted to know whom and what it was for.

"It's for you," Charlie told him. "It's your share of the deal I put through with my code wire."

It seems that he had made quite a haul on a stock transaction. But Warden Moyer did not like that a bit. He declined the check and gave him hell. He even threatened to lock him up. Charlie did not mind the blasting. It was like water on a duck's back for him. But he was never permitted to send out another code wire. Not from that United States Penitentiary, at any rate.

Perhaps, it didn't make much difference to him. He had all the money he wanted. Seven or more million dollars, they said. Anyway, he did not stay there much longer. He was doing a 15-year stretch. But he had no intention of serving it in full.

It is a matter of public knowledge that he had hired Harry M. Daugherty, of President Harding's cabinet fame as his lawyer. Nobody knows how much he paid him. But, years later, according to the newspapers, Daugherty still claimed that Morse was indebted to him for $50,000.

Daugherty looked after the Washington end of Morse's case. Charlie began to eat soap and other stuff and soon developed the symptoms of locomotor ataxia or of Bright's disease. I don't remember which. And it does not matter after all. But he was certified in a hopeless condition and in immediate danger of his life. They transferred him to Fort Oglethorpe, Ga. A few months later, he was pardoned by President Taft, after having served, all together, a little over two years on a 15-year sentence. Once released, naturally he declined to die. He must have lived another dozen years or so.

I remained in Atlanta till the expiration of my full term and served an extra month for the fine. I was not paroled. In fact, for some reason or other which I do not remember, I did not apply for a parole, notwithstanding my good behavior. I was released unconditionally in July 1912. No effort was made to deport me.

CHAPTER VII

"PAGE MR. INSULL!" OR THE PONZI POWER, LIGHT & WATER COMPANY OF BLOCTON, ALA.

My meeting in Peachtree Street with the two Secret Service men convinced me that Atlanta, as the gag goes, was "no place for a minister's son." As a matter of fact, like the rest of Georgia, it was no place for anybody except a native "cracker". The Ku Klux Klan was very active. The streets of Marietta were still spattered with the blood of Leo Frank.

I made myself scarce p.d.q., and even quicker than that. "When the midnight choo-choo blew for Alabam," I was on it. Why Alabama of all places? For no other reason than that Alabama was in a western direction. "Go West, young man, go West!"

A few years later, astrologers told me it was all wrong. I should never have gone West. My stars pointed to the East, they said. And they were right. To become enlightened, a man ought to travel always in the direction of the sun. Every yap knows that. But, on the other hand, the eastern routes are so crowded with blue lodge members that a traveler must sit up all night to get to a railroad ticket-window ahead of them.

Be that as it may, I landed in Birmingham, I could not miss it. That is unless I catapulted from the train. And I wouldn't have missed it if I had missed it. The only thing of interest I found there was a "quack." An old acquaintance of mine from Providence.

This quack had an infirmary. Whether or not he had a license to practice is a horse of a different color. Maybe he did and, yet, maybe he didn't. Away back in Providence he did not have one. In fact, he had to leave in a hurry on account of that. But in Birmingham he might have had one. If he did, I don't know how he got it, because the only "medi cine" he had ever taken in was castor oil when he was a kid.

I saw his sign over the infirmary and was attracted by the name. It was familiar. Out of curiosity, I went in to find out whether it was a case of two practitioners with an identical shingle or of two shingles for one and the same "doctor". The moment I saw the man, the recognition was mutual.

We talked. He was very frank about his activities. Couldn't very well have been anything else with me. The infirmary was a "racket," he explained. A good racket He was cleaning up! With what? With fake claims against the coal mining companies!

This is how he worked it. He had agents scattered all over. In every mining camp. They were on a commission basis. As soon as a miner was the victim of some accident, especially a minor accident, he would be coached by the quack's agent to exaggerate the injury, to make it appear an internal injury, and to decline any settlement that may be offered by the company.

Right away, or in due course of time, according to the nature of the injury, the victim would end up at the quack's infirmary. He would stay there weeks or maybe months, leading the life of Riley. Nothing was too good for him. The quack would report his condition to the company and vouch for any sort of internal injury. Eventually, a settlement had to be discussed. This invariably included doctor's fees and infirmary bills at figures which would have staggered even a Johns Hopkins or Mayo clinic's patient. Plus this, the company had to pay some damages to the man himself. The quack cut in 50-50 on the damages too.

The infirmary was always full. And why wouldn't it be? When genuine accidents were scarce, fake accidents were resorted to. A miner would get his "buddy" to throw a few lumps of coal at him. They would pile up some "slack." Summon help. And report a "cave in." The miner would claim minor injuries. The quack would certify to them and collect. And that goes to show that Barnum was right. There is a sucker born every day, and they make him claim adjuster for a coal mining company! It surely is "a great life if you don't weaken!"

I had a splendid chance to get in that accident racket. I was offered a job. Not for my superficial knowledge of medicine. Rather, for any intimate knowledge of the quack's methods and past. But I am no blackmailer. I live and let live. Besides, that infirmary looked to me as if it might lead me to a relapse. That is, to one of those Alabama chain-gangs. And I gave it a wide berth.

I went to Blocton, instead, - a mining town with a sizable number of Italians where I figured that my knowledge of English might come in handy. In fact, I managed to eke out a living, sometimes acting as interpreter; others, helping, the local storekeepers out with their books; occasionally as a male nurse to some battered miner.

Life was far from dull in that small community. Between christenings, weddings and other celebrations, we had more good times than we would have in a large city. It was like one big, happy family. A real brotherhood of common interests and endeavors and of neighborly love. Men, women and children were all banded together by a uniform hope in and fear of their lord and master, the capricious King Coal. Gaiety ebbed or flowed in that camp at the king's whim, according to whether he was lavish or the other way, with tons of precious black mineral or with his frightful destruction of human lives!

It was in my capacity of male nurse that I soon discovered something amiss in that community. There was no running water. No electric current. The water was toted from wells and springs. Candles and kerosene furnished the light. To administer first aid under those handicaps was no cinch. Yet, it had to be done because the hospital was two miles away and the only way to get there was to walk.

I made up my mind that the camp must be provided with both light and running water. "To decide" with me is "to act." Even in those days I was no slouch at promoting. For the very good reason that money with me is always the last consideration instead of being the first. Why should I worry about the money? The money is always around to be had. The main thing is to have an idea. A plausible idea which can be dressed up and sold.

All I needed for that water and power plant were a gasoline engine, a pump, a dynamo and a tank. The camp was on a slope of a hill. On top of the hill and down part of the other slope, there was another small, but more exclusive district for the native population. At the bottom of that slope was a creek. The whole community was organized under a charter and had some sort of a town council.

It didn't take much to get a town meeting called. A notice was posted. Word passed around. And one Sunday afternoon we all gathered in the town hall. I was introduced and took the floor.

"Gentlemen," I said, "let's not waste any time in idle words. We are all here to discuss the ways and means and expediency of providing every house in this community with running water and electric light. I have made a superficial survey of the proposition and found that it would be practical to pump the water from the creek to a tank on top of the hill and distribute it from there. The same engine which runs the pump, could also run the dynamo for the electric current. I have no figures to submit at this time as to the cost of the plant, the piping and the wiring. I have no money to pay for it."

"What I propose to do is to get an estimate of the cost. Then I will form a corporation asking each member of this community to subscribe to one or more shares of its preferred stock. Enough of it to pay for the cost. I intend to retain a controlling interest of the common stock for my own services and sell the balance to cover overheads and other emergency expenses of the corporation."

"The rates for water and electric current will be determined by the town council as soon as I shall be able to submit figures for the running cost of the plant and the amortization of the preferred stock. I expect those rates to leave a reasonable margin of profit for the common stock. While I am desirous to promote the welfare of this community, I feel that I am entitled to some returns for my time, energy and services."

"Just now, I ask that a resolution be put to a vote of this meeting endorsing my activities and endeavors and directing the town council to give me a deed to the land needed for the power plant and water tank and a franchise to run pipes and wires. I thank you."

The resolution was unanimously adopted. A few days later, I was given the franchise at a special meeting of the town council. I had a power equipment company send down a couple of engineers to lay out the whole thing and give me some figures. In another month or so, the plant would have materialized.

But . . . something happened to upset my plans. Something always happens! It never fails. Something so entirely unexpected that it always catches me unaware. Like a flower pot that lands on a man's head from a three-story window.

That time, it was an accident. Not to me. To one of the nurses at the company's hospital. Pearl Gossett was her name. She had been cooking a patient's meal on a gasoline stove. The stove exploded. She was frightfully burned. The entire left arm and part of her breast and shoulder were actually one mass of charred flesh.

A couple of days after the accident, Dr. Thomas, the company's doctor, came over to the camp. We were very friendly. He never failed to call on me whenever he was at the camp. He did not fail that day. He stopped at the house where I was staying and we drank a bottle of beer. Our conversation drifted to the nurse.

"How's Pearl?" I inquired. "Is she making any progress?"

"Her condition is very serious," the doctor said. "Almost desperate. Gangrene is setting in."

"Can't anything be done to save her?" I asked.

"Skin grafting, perhaps," he replied. "I wanted to try it. But I can't find anybody who will give up as little as an inch of his skin for her."

He told me he had asked everybody around the camp. He had been turned down in each instance.

It did not seem fair that a young girl like Pearl should be permitted to die such a horrible death. That nurse had been so kind to her patients that it seemed inconceivable she should meet with such ingratitude. It made my blood sizzle to think that any person could be so selfish, so cowardly as to refuse a mere inch of his own skin to save a human life.

"How many inches of skin do you need altogether, doctor?" I asked him.

"Forty of fifty, I guess," he said. "But I can't find even ten in a community of 2,000 or more people."

"You're all wrong, doctor," I said. "You have found them. I will give all the skin you need."

"You?" he said as if he was afraid he had misunderstood.

"You? You will give the whole of it?"

"Yes, doctor," I confirmed, "I will. When do you want me?"

"We cannot put the thing off very long," he answered.

"But I don't want to hurry you either. You might want to prepare for it. Sort of brace up. When can you be ready?"

"I am ready now," I told him.

Dr. Thomas took a good took at me before he replied. He wanted to make sure I wouldn't flinch. Evidently, what he saw in my eyes decided him.

"All right, then. Come along," he said. "But you better put your coat on," he added with a twinkle in his eyes, noticing that in my eagerness to follow him, I was going in my shirt sleeves.

That evening, I was put on the operating table. Before they gave me the ether, I wanted to know from what part of the body they were going to peel my skin.

"From the thigh, said Dr. Thomas. "By the way, from which leg shall we take it?" he asked.

"It's all the same to me," I told him. "Take it from both, if you need it."

And he did. When I came to, both of my legs were bandaged, from hip to knee. And sore! Oh, boy! But what's a couple of sore legs more or less between friends? Just a trifle! In fact, I was in the hospital the best part of the next three months. Convalescing? No. Shedding more skin on the installment plan. Enough to make a couple of suit-cases. But I say that with no regret. It was probably instrumental in saving that nurse's life. If not her life, her arm. In either case, I am glad to have done something to help a fellow being. Regardless of what it may have cost me.

Undoubtedly, I suffered physically. The ordeal was quite painful. Also, I incurred some danger from complications. Pneumonia, for instance. But I did not get anything worse than pleurisy. Economically, it just blew my power plant to smithereens! But again I may say: What's a power plant more or less in the land Of Insull? A trifle! A mere trifle! He did not miss it! And neither did I. Not much.

CHAPTER VIII

MR. PONZI'S MEDICAL CAREER IN MOBILE IS ABRUPTLY CUT SHORT BY A UNIVERSITY PRESIDENT.

It was around the Spring or Summer of 1914 that I made my appearance in Mobile, Ala. I had come from Pensacola on the coast-wise steamer Tarpon. Not as a passenger. Only as a painter. On a contract job to paint the deck structure.

I did what I was supposed to do. But had some trouble collecting what was owed to me. I quarreled with the Captain. Told him to go to blazes. He went back to Pensacola, instead. I remained in Mobile.

In those days, one place was just as good as the next. I had discovered that I could paint - more or less. Signs were my specialty. Any kind of signs. But I could figure on a house painting job, too, and manage to make a living almost anywhere. I would work one town and shift to the next one without any trouble.

In Mobile I did fairly well at the beginning. Then things slacked up a little. But as I was getting ready to move on, I noticed an ad in the local papers.

"Librarian wanted at the Medical College. Apply in person," it read. I applied. Knowing the Greek language, those big medical words were not exactly "all Greek to me." They were something I understood. So I landed the job. Which did not pay much, but I took it because it was dignified and congenial, so to speak. Not many would cherish it like I did, eating their noon lunch in an anatomical room full of corpses pickled in formaldehyde, with possibility of picking up a slice off someone's thigh, instead of a slice of boiled ham.

Speaking of congeniality, I had all sorts of pranks played on me by those medical students. Some of the boys were really cute in their ways! They would just as soon as not drop a test-tube full of typhoid germs into my soup. Or turn loose in the library a whole cage of guinea pig injected with cholera morbus. Anything to provoke a laugh. One night, after a storm, which had put the lights out of commission, I turned in, in the dark. My room was on the ground floor of the building. The moment I got under the sheets, I felt the presence of someone else in my bed. A drunken student, I thought. But it wasn't. It was a "stiff" - a dead Negro - embalmed, too. As I could not carry him alone up to the second floor where he belonged, I laid him on the floor in my room. We both slept peacefully, but I woke up first. Such was life at the college. One prank after another. But it worked both ways.

My duties as librarian were the least of all. I catalogued the ten thousand or more books in the library, and the periodicals, too. I observed regular hours and issued books. I collaborated also on the college publication. Typed the whole of it. Showed visitors around the building. And, nights included I was tied up with the free out-patient obstetric service.

In this connection, when a call came in from an expectant mother, it was up to me to hunt up the two students assigned to the case - who, by the way, might be anywhere except home, - prepare their satchel, send them on their way. Sometimes it happened that one of the two students could not be found, or would not be found. Then I would turn into a midwife and go along myself. There was nothing to it. Nearly all were ordinary deliveries, not "special" deliveries. And, between attending classes, reading up text books, watching operations and postmortems, etc., I knew as much about deliveries as any of the boys, in fact, as much as any mail carrier. After all, it was only a question of waiting. I could not improve upon nature. It would have to take its course. And it usually did, sooner or later. And the waiting was not half as hard on me as it was on the expectant mother.

All considered, that job suited me fine. I got along capitally with the faculty and the boys. I liked Mobile, its bay, the well-known Mobile Bay, its climate, everything. But my contentment did not last over a year. I should have known it wouldn't last. If it had, it would have interrupted a long circle of bad breaks.

Before I proceed to narrate the events, I must explain that the Medical College was a part of the University of Alabama.

The university itself was located at Tuscaloosa. The Medical College was located at Mobile, instead of in the campus, because a medical college always needs to be where it may have easy access to a fairly large hospital. Mobile, being a larger city than Tuscaloosa, afforded better hospital facilities.

I do not recollect what had caused the Medical College to locate in Mobile instead of in Birmingham. All I know is that it was there and that, in my time, a bunch of Birmingham doctors were trying their darndest to have it removed from Mobile to their city. The Mobile M.D.'s were pulling their own political wires just as hard to have the college stay down there. The moment I became connected with that institution, my loyalty to the faculty, naturally, led me to side with them. But it was not within the scope of my job to take an active part in the controversy, except in my capacity of collaborator in the college publication. As such, I worked hand in hand with one of the faculty.

He and I were real "buddies" in that fight. He was the most rabid opponent the Birmingham bunch ever had to contend with. At least, that's what we all believed. We banked on him. We had implicit confidence in his loyalty and sincerity, until something happened to shake our confidence in him.

It was the night before he was leaving for his summer vacation. He and I were alone in his office. He was straightening out his papers. Giving me some instructions; arranging things in general. And when he got ready to leave the building, he handed me two letters to mail.

"Be sure to mail them tonight," he told me, "because I am leaving on the morning train in the same direction and I want them to get to destination before me."

I had no intention of disregarding his wishes. As soon as he left the building, I got ready to do the same thing and to go to the post-office. But I happened to glance at the envelopes. I noticed that one was addressed to a doctor in Birmingham notoriously active in the projected removal of the Medical College from Mobile. The other was addressed to the President of the university, whom we had reason to suspect was antagonistic to the Mobile crowd. I was thunderstruck. From what I knew, that faculty member was the last one who should ever have anything to do with such people. He and they were supposed to be at logger-heads.

I was a bit perplexed. There was something before me, which did not look right. Yet it seemed inconceivable to suspect him of treachery. I did not know what to do. But my loyalty to the institution prevailed. I decided to open those letters. I could always seal them again and mail them if they contained 'no' treasonable matter.

I opened them. Read them. And there, before me was the evidence that he had been double-crossing the college right along. He was working hand-in-hand with the Birmingham bunch.

My course was clear. I could not suppress that evidence and remain loyal to the college. I saw no reason for suppressing it anyway. Since he was a double-crosser, I owed him nothing. Let him face the consequences.

I called up Dr. Frazer, then acting-dean, and told him to come right over to the college. He did. I showed him the letters. He asked me to make copies of them, and took the originals. The following morning the derelict faculty member was asked to resign. He did not and could not decline to do so, under the circumstances.

Within a few days, the matter was reported to the President of the University. The faculty, of course, did not fail to express their chagrin at having discovered that he was siding with the Birmingham crowd. They felt that he should have been neutral. I don't know what he replied, but he made it a point to direct that I be fired.

Dr. Frazer showed me his letter. I laughed. Told him not to pay any attention to it, that the man who wrote it was crazy with the heat.

"But he is my superior in the University," said Dr. Frazer, "I must obey him."

"Not in this instance. But go ahead, if you want to," I told him. "Only you'd better warn him that if I am fired I'll bring suit and let the world know the reason I am being fired."

"I can't tell him that," protested Dr. Frazer. "He expects me to tell him that I have fired you."

"Well, it's just too bad about him," I insisted. "You can just tell him - that I am not fired and that I won't be fired. On second thought, I believe I will spare you even that trouble. In the morning I will give you a letter from me to send along. If after that, he still insists that I be fired, it will be time enough for you to act."

I did write the delinquent faculty member of the University a letter. And what a letter! Insulting? Of course, not. Only diplomatic. But I had him in a corner and I let him have it. He had it coming, anyway. The result was that I was not fired. Not right away. He got rid of me in another way, though. That is, by failing to appropriate any money for my salary. And so, before the summer was over, I was out of that job, after all.

CHAPTER IX

MR. PONZI PULLS A FAST ONE ON THE NEW ORLEANS CITIZENRY AND DUCKS NONE TOO SOON.

From Mobile I went to New Orleans just in time to witness the terrible hurricane of September 1915. "Witness" is no word. I was right in the midst of it! Everything was flying but the birds! Store-signs, shingles, tiles, tree-limbs, galvanized iron-roofs! In Esplanade Avenue the trees were bending like blades of grass! I never saw the like of it before or since. It remained the worst storm in the history of the city until Huey Long struck New Orleans. His antics made it look like a breeze in comparison. As a political twister, Huey couldn't be beaten on this side of hell by either man or elements!

In New Orleans, Tulane did not need a librarian. They could have used me as a scorekeeper. But I could not keep myself, much less a whole score. As a half-back, it was entirely out of the question. I wouldn't have known what to do with the other half while one half was playing.

So, I reverted to painting. The good old reliable vocation. The only steady and permanent job. More permanent than a permanent wave.

Most store-signs had been blown by the storm to Baton Rouge and points North. It was cheaper for the store-keepers to have new ones painted than to move their stores up there after the old ones. I worked, they worked, we worked. And, by Mardi Gras, New Orleans again looked the same as it had looked for the past couple of centuries, only a little more spic and span on account of the fresh paint. I had those signs as flashy and bright as a Creole.

So far as appearances went, everything was normal by Spring. Only, the storm seemed to have kindled old feuds along the waterfront and around the market district. Hardly a week passed without some shooting, or some stabbing, or both. Blood flowed more freely than water. Life in New Orleans began to look like one murder after another. Things were so bad that people were selling their houses to buy cemetery lots.

It was after the wholesale slaughter in front of the Monte Leone Hotel that an Italian Protestant minister and I, were commenting on the situation, at his house, over the supper table. We were both very indignant Such a state of affairs put the entire Italian colony in a bad light. The press was yelling blue murder as usual, and demanding action. The Mayor was pulling his few stray hairs and wishing his constituents would behave themselves until after election. The police were following imaginary clues, which led nowhere. Chasing rainbows. Chasing everything but the culprits. And the killers were nonchalantly oiling their guns and honing their stilettos.

The Italian minister and I were in complete accord that something ought to be done. But who was going to do it? Huey Long wasn't there yet. And nobody else knew where to start from or what to do. Except burying the dead. The mortality was so great that National Casket shares soared out of sight on the exchange. Insurance companies were on the verge of bankruptcy, while undertakers were buying apartment houses. We decided to step into the fray and throw a monkey wrench into the feudist's ranks.

The two of us, in size and weight, could not have licked more than a couple of sheets of postage stamps without running out of breath. We were no Carneras. However, what we lacked in muscular development and boxing technique we possessed in ingenuity and practical psychology. We knew the killers were bold because they felt secure from detection. And why wouldn't they be? The cops, as cops go, couldn't detect a wisp of smoke even if they were sitting on a bon-fire. Informers were scarcer than flying elephants. Nobody dared to squeal. Not even the pigs. But let the fear grow among the killers that they might be secretly denounced by persons whose identity they could not establish, and they would undoubtedly slow up. That's what the minister and I thought, because nothing deters a man from evil more than the certainty or a strong probability of being caught at it and punished for it.

With all of our wisdom, the minister and I were a couple of nuts, so to speak. Full of crazy ideas. We were about the same age and had much in common. He knew I couldn't paint any better than he could preach.

He knew he couldn't preach any worse than I could paint. Our religious views did not clash. He was a Protestant. I was a Catholic. But he didn't give a "darn" what I believed in. And. I didn't give a "damn" what he believed in. All considered, we were like two peas in a pod. Two bodies with one soul.

Having reached unanimous conclusions on the subject of the killings, we decided to act. We pulled one of the craziest stunts ever conceived. Actually took our lives into our own hands. No doubt about that. If word had got around in that community connecting us with what we did, we would have been stuffed with more lead than a fisherman's sinker.

We constituted ourselves as a committee of two, allegedly the spokesmen of a newly organized secret society, which existed only in our fervid imagination. On the stroke of midnight we slipped mysteriously into the city editor's office of the New Orleans States and whispered to him to lead us somewhere where we could converse in all privacy. It was a matter of life and death, we told him. He believed it. A matter of his own life and death, he thought perhaps, by the looks of us two. But he decided that the safest way for him was to humor us. To gain time until he could find out whether he was dealing with a couple of lunatics on a furlough from the bug-house, or with a couple of murderers, or with two good men with a real story.

He led us to a little room. Made us sit down.

"Spill it," he said, using a verb that would cover the situation from all angles. It was clear that we were there to "spill" something. But he didn't know for sure whether it was a story or his blood. And he felt that the quickest way to find out was to use a verb, which would compel us to show our hand.

"Not so fast my dear Sir," I warned him. "Before we speak we must have your word that you will never disclose our identity under any circumstances. If it became known that we have come to you, we would be killed in no time. Will you give us your word?"

"Yes, I can do that. I will give you my word that I will never divulge your identity to anyone," he promised. "But what's the story?" he asked.

"The story is this," I told him. "The better element of the Italian colony have decided to take matters into their own hands and put an end to all of these killings. They have organized a secret society and pledged every member to gather information about every person suspected to be connected with any murder. The information will be turned in daily to the executive officers of the society, pieced together and transmitted to the police. The secret society will have spies everywhere."

"Who are the members of the society?" the editor asked.

"That, we cannot disclose. A fairly large number of Italians attended the first meeting and took the pledge. They came a few at a time and a at different hours so as not to arouse curiosity. They conferred with the leaders. Took their pledge. Learned the passwords. And left a few at a time as they had come. This is as much as we can tell you," I replied to the editor.

"What about yourselves?" he inquired.

"We have been delegated to represent the society and communicate with the press, the authorities and the police. Our first call has been for you. We will arrange later to meet the Mayor and the Chief of Police. We have brought a copy of a resolution adopted at the first meeting of the society. Here is the copy," I said handing it to him. It was a resolution the minister and I had drafted after supper. The editor took it and read it.

"That's swell!" he said. "I am going to print it as it is on the front page of tomorrow's morning edition. Who is it signed by?" he asked looking at the signatures.

"By us," I answered. "The Reverend here as the executive secretary of the society. I as its executive director. But you must not publish our names."

"Of course not," he agreed. "I'll cut the signatures off before the copy leaves my hands."

We lingered in the editor's office long enough to be complimented for our high-spirited sense of civic duties. And make a few arrangements too. We told the editor we would be glad to meet both the Mayor and the Chief of Police. But couldn't risk being seen either at the City Hall or at headquarters.

"You ring me up in the morning," he suggested. "Ill speak to the Mayor and the Chief and have them meet you anywhere."

The following morning the New Orleans States came out with a front-page article on our midnight call. It painted us as two potential martyrs for the cause of "law and order." Only, that they did not exactly use the same words that made Cal Coolidge as famous as the beer did Milwaukee. They said something else to the same effect. Praised the predominantly law-abiding element of the Italian colony. Published the entire resolution, minus the signatures. Thank God for that! The minister and I had been up all night waiting for a copy of the States to make sure that we were not named. If our names had been mentioned, dawn would have found us en route for parts unknown.

The story was a scoop which made the city editors of the Times-Picayune and other papers sizzle in their editorial chairs. There was more swearing around their offices that morning than at an atheist congress.

Reporters were aroused from their slumbers and rushed to the Italian district. Told to come back with a story or not at all. Promised all sorts of bonuses if they brought in a real whopper. But where could they land a story? They might as well have gone down to the seashore and interviewed a whole clam colony. The Italians, as a rule, are very tight lipped. But on that occasion, the New Orleans Italians were even more so. In the first place they had nothing to say, because they didn't know anymore about the whole thing than the reporters did. Then, they were scared to death to open their mouths.

In fact, they were in a pickle. They couldn't deny to be members of the secret society without permitting inference that they sided with the criminal element. They could not admit of being members without risking their lives. They were in a jam no matter which way they turned.

To make matters worse, every darned one of them believed in the existence of this imaginary society. Yet, everyone realized that he had been left out. If he was a good citizen, he was worried. He felt that he had been left out because he was suspected to be bad. If he was a bad citizen, there was no question in his mind that he was also under suspicion. And, not only was he worried, but he was scared.

The reverend and I didn't realize what it was going to be like until we took our usual walk down the Italian district. It was almost pathetic to watch some of those people. Men ordinarily talkative and sociable had shut down like clams and were rude. Or, they spoke in whispers. Constantly, they were looking over their back, perhaps. With a sober look in their face, they would meet in the street and exchange signs. Signs that were soundless questions and answers. Peculiar of the southern

Italians. But which spoke volumes. Volumes of fear and anxiety over a situation beyond their comprehension.

The minister and I did not hang around the district very long. We couldn't. Knowing what we knew, it was an awful strain for us to keep from bursting out laughing. But a mere smile would have been fatal. It would have doomed us. That district had lost all sense of humor. We had to go home to relax. And to phone to out friend the editor.

We called him up. The Mayor wanted to see us, he said. Wanted to thank us for what we had done. And the Chief likewise. He was very anxious to confer with us. Both wanted to know when and where they could meet us. We suggested an appointment. The editor picked us up in his car and drove out of the city somewhere. There we met another car with the Mayor and the Chief. The Chief was driving it.

The cars turned into a side road and stopped. We all alighted and were introduced. Then we talked. The conference lasted about an hour. It was mostly with the Chief. We had to arrange with him so that we could make daily reports of the society's activities. He gave us a phone number and some sort of a pass-word to identify ourselves. He said there would always be somebody at the end of the wire to take our messages. He offered us police protection. But we refused it. We couldn't very well give the police a chance to find out that we were a couple of fakes.

The Mayor didn't say much. Except promising his full cooperation. And we were willing to let it go at that. But the editor butted in. He suggested that the city appropriate some money to help the society in its investigation. The Mayor jumped at the suggestion. It did not involve any of his money, anyway. He said he would have $30,000 available for it right away. Just think of it! He was ready to throw 30,000 bucks right in our lap! The minister and I thanked him effusively for his generosity. But, actually, we got sort of panicky. To accept money under these circumstances would have been entirely too dangerous.

The conference broke up. We went home to talk things over. They had gone too far, we decided. What were we going to do with it? We did not want that money or any money.

We were just a couple of madcaps. Not swindlers. But how could we refuse the money and still appear genuine?

The more we discussed the situation, the more we became convinced that it was fraught with danger. One little slip and we would be sunk.

"Let's scram," I suggested. "This burg is getting uncomfortable."

"Together?" the reverend asked.

"Not on your life," I replied. "I like you and all that but you and I are just like nitric acid and glycerin. If you keep them separate, they are harmless. But if you mix them, there is hell to pay."

We parted. The minister solicited and obtained an immediate transfer to some other distant pastorate. I accepted a job as a foreign salesman for a motor truck company in Wichita Falls, Texas. The Mayor, the Chief of Police and the city editor of the New Orleans States were left to pull their own chestnuts out of the fire. I have never bothered since to find out what they thought of us. Whether they ever discovered that they were duped. If they haven't they know it now. But I might as well tell them also that it was done out of mischief and not out of malice. I hope they can take a joke.

CHAPTER X

FROM THE COPIOUS CROP OF AMERICAN BLOSSOMS MR. PONZI PICKS HIMSELF AN EXQUISITE ROSE OF THE AMERICAN BEAUTY VARIETY AS HIS LIFE'S EMBLEM.

In Wichita Falls, Texas, I got my first training as a foreign correspondent and salesman. The company I was working for manufactured auto-trucks. Shipped them everywhere. Had agents or users in almost every country in the world. Except, of course, Germany and her allies.

All of our foreign business was transacted by mail or by cable. In the English, French, Italian, Spanish or Portuguese language. And it required us to keep posted on shipping routes and rates. On custom tariffs abroad. On foreign currencies and exchange. On postal and telegraph rates. All knowledge which, later, played such an important part in the most spectacular episode of my career in America.

Life in Wichita Falls was not very exciting. The factory was about two miles from the city itself. On the edge of a prairie section, typical of the South-west. Not far from the Oklahoma state line. I boarded a stone-throw from the office. And, often, I worked after hours because I had no place to go.

The only exciting thing about the place was a bear. Not of the Max variety, either. Just a big, grown bear. I don't remember whether it belonged to the watchman or the manager. But I know we had a cage for it in front of the building. And I know that after hours the watchman would turn it loose for it while and let it roam around. That bear never failed to walk right in my office, upstairs, and scare the wits out of me. It would sneak in without making any noise. As if it wore rubber shoes. Then, all of a sudden, I would hear its breath right in the back of my chair or catch a glimpse of it as it was rounding the corner of my desk. And I would jump. And swear.

I couldn't argue with it, or shoo it away. I would just duck and shut the door. I have no use for that kind of of pets, for overgrown pets that can slap me from one end of the room to the other. There is nothing cute about that sort of animal, except the smell. In that respect, a good size bear can shame a dozen pole cats.

The Wichita Falls Motor Truck Company was owned by Kemp and Kell. I don't know this day who Kemp and Kell were. Off hand, I would say they were an alias for Wichita Falls. They owned everything in sight. What Kemp did not own, Kell did. And vice versa. But I can't say for sure whether they were humans or just a myth. I never saw either one. On the other hand, I have never seen "America's Richest" either. Yet, there is plenty of evidence of his presence in the States. Gasoline stations, A & P stores, the National City Bank, and so forth. Anyway, whenever dimes get scarce, you can bet your shirt he has been around your neighborhood. That man keeps the mint working overtime to restock the dime supply. They claim he gives them out again as souvenirs. But it looks as if for every one he gives away he sinks a hundred for himself.

Speaking of millionaires, in Wichita Falls I had a chance of becoming a multi-millionaire like him. A perfectly good chance. Hundreds of millions of dollars were made in that section after I left. Oil deposits were discovered. Wells drilled. Gushers set off and harnessed. But the oil deposits were there in my time too. Amply in evidence. Only, I was too blind to notice the evidence.

In fact, we used to spend some week-ends in that section which is known today as the Burke Burnett Oil Field. A truck load of us clerks would drive there Saturday afternoons with a good supply of bottled beer and eatables. We would spend the night in the open air. On the prairies. In day time, we would hunt cotton-tail rabbits and bull frogs to add to our bill of fare.

The frogs were in the many pools of water which were scattered all around the prairies. The water of those pools was streaked all over with oil. The iridescent patches of floating oil were everywhere. And where else would that oil come from, but from underground deposits? But I never stopped to think of it. If I had, I could have bought that whole section at five dollars an acre! Yet, that land covers enough oil to make it worth the price of real estate in down-town New York.

I left Wichita Falls, minus the millions, in January 1917 to go to Boston as a foreign correspondent for an export Company. A sort of a gamble on futures, because the job didn't pay much. But the prospects looked good. The company was doing very well, for itself. And it was quite lavish with its employees. With promises. The only trouble was that its promises did not pay our living expenses. But, by starving one day and eating a little less the next one, we employees always managed, more or less, to keep handsomely in debt.

Although my job with the company was not what you may call a bonanza, it was a source of some satisfaction to me. It made me realize that, after 13 years in America, I had reached the point where I needed no longer to turn to menial jobs. I was in every respect equipped to fill an office position. Especially with a firm engaged in foreign trade. So, even if my job didn't pay much, I kept at it to acquire additional experience, to meet new people, to build myself up a wide acquaintance. Eventually, I intended to branch out for myself.

By then I was 35 years old. A sort of happy-go-lucky fellow with a penchant for good times. A little lonesome now and then. When I realized that I had no home of my own. But otherwise care-free. And rather partial to good looking girls. I liked them all, God bless them! In a sort of good fellowship way. You know how it is. Never giving a thought that in the same community, within a few blocks from where I was rooming lived the girl whom a kind fate-kind to me-had destined to be my wife.

It was the night before Memorial Day. Around midnight. I had been to the Pop's and was waiting for a streetcar at the Boylston Street subway station. An elderly lady was with me.

A beautiful girl, escorted by a young man, was, like us, waiting for the same car. She could not have been there long, because I know I would have sensed her presence. The same as I felt myself drawn to turn and glance in her direction the moment she set her foot on the subway platform.

One glance at her, at that picture of loveliness and kindness and clean vivacity . . . One look into her deep, dark, smiling eyes . . . At that pretty, round face, framed in a background of gorgeous curls . . . At her whole fascinating ensemble . . . And I was no longer able to remove my eyes from her. I remained there, staring so intently that for my unrepressed and evident feeling of respectful admiration, I might have appeared rude.

I have no idea how long I stood there looking at that girl. Probably, only a matter of seconds. But they could have been hours and I wouldn't have known the difference. Time, space, the world and everything else around me, except that girl, had ceased to exist.

The lady who was with me must have noticed my state of blissful reverie and followed the direction of my glances, because not only did she see the girl, but recognized her too.

"Why, there is Rose!" she said to me. "I want you to meet her Mr. Ponzi. She was one of my pupils."

We walked up to the couple.

"Rose," said the lady speaking to her. "I want you to meet Mr. Ponzi." then turned to me. "This is Miss Gnecco," she said.

"How do you do?" the girl acknowledging the introduction with a voice as sweet as her looks.

"How do you do?" I returned, but I made no effort to conceal how I felt. I didn't care who knew how I felt. In fact, I wanted the whole world to know that I had met the girl of my dreams and surrendered unconditionally to her charms.

She lived in Somerville. Not very far from where I lived. So, we were in the same street-car for the next twenty minutes or so. She was with her escort a couple of seats ahead of us, on the right. All the way to Somerville, my eyes did not leave her a minute.

When we got home, the lady I was escorting asked me what I thought of that girl.

"I think she is wonderful!" I replied. "I am going to marry her."

"Why, Mr. Ponzi!" the lady said. "You must be crazy!"

"I am. I am crazy about that girl," I admitted and that was no exaggeration.

Eight months later Rose and I were married at "a little church around the corner" in Vine Street, Somerville. She has been my companion ever since. The faithful, loyal, little wife who has never faltered in the many days of sorrow and adversity. The one inspiration that has enabled me to face the most crucial crises of my life with a heart steeled by our reciprocal love.

Rose is the most precious gift America could have tendered me. She was born and raised in the United States. In Boston. I am grateful and thankful to America for the gift. My wife is ample reward for everything I have suffered, justly or unjustly, during the 31 years in the United States. I cannot bear any grudge, any malice, against a country which has been so lavish and generous as to place within my reach to pick, from a whole garden-full of beautiful flowers, such as American girls are, what has been for me the most exquisite of all blossoms. An American Beauty. My Rose!

CHAPTER XI

SCHOOL STREET, BOSTON, SCENE OF THE EXPLOSION THAT WAS HEARD AROUND THE WORLD.

"The shot that was heard around the world," was fired on the bridge between Lexington and Concord. Some shot! I hope to tell it was some shot! If the bullet had gone all the way around the world with the sound, the man who fired that shot would have been killed backwards by his own bullet. That's going some. Even for a Lucky Strike radio sketch. But, on the other hand, "Vas you dere, Charlie?" No, baron. I must admit I wasn't there. And nowhere near it.

That shot has no immediate relation to this story. It was fired away back. At the time when Paul Revere could still make his morning canters, minus the entourage of every city or town official from the North End to Lexington. At the time when the Dawes boys were still smoking their corn-cobs upside up. Instead of French briars upside down. And were filling them with tobacco that didn't come from the R. F. C.

But, if the shot that was heard around the world has no immediate relation to this story, it has a remote relation to it as a question of acoustic range. Because the explosion of what is known as my "financial bubble" was also heard around the world. It was recorded by every seismograph beneath the Stratosphere. And it made history for School Street. The same as the shot made it for Lexington and Concord.

School Street is one of Boston's oldest landmarks. It has been there ever since houses were built on both sides of it. Until a few years, ago, it was short, narrow and congested. Now, it is still short. And congested. But not quite so narrow, from the waist up. That is, toward Tremont Street. It has been widened. Pot-bellied politicians, in transit to and from the City Hall, couldn't get by without being squeezed. And there is nothing a politician hates more than being squeezed.

Once upon a while, School Street was famous. For its historical buildings. The Parker House, for instance. At the corner of Tremont Street. Noted for its Boston "Tea" parties. Past, but not remote. And present. But, whereas tea was tea in the days gone by, it's just plain whiskey today. Or gin. Or both.

Ever since the demise of the old Copley Square Hotel and of brother Spraklin's regime, the Parker House has become the political headquarters of Greater Boston. All shades of Democrats and Republicans can be found there, in the various stages of ascent or descent. And in some awful combinations too.

Other venerable buildings in School Street are the little church, on the opposite corner from the Parker House, the Five-Cents Saving Bank, and last, but not the least, the City Hall. I can't say much about the church. I don't know enough about it. I have never been in it. But it's sort of exclusive. Maybe, on account of its denomination. Like a $10,000 bill.

The Five-Cents Savings Bank is there and yet it isn't. It was there in my time. With a School Street frontage. Today, it's around the corner in Province Street. Someone said that it moved there out of pure snobbery. On account of too much riff-raff across the street; where I had my office. The officials used to get heart failure regularly, watching the long line of people who were bringing to my office the savings they had just withdrawn from the bank. And they turned the building around and made it face the other way.

The City Hall is what it has always been. A bone of contention for the Democrats. It has been responsible for more caesarean incisions in the Democratic Party than any other political plum. Usually, there are from a dozen to a score of candidates for the Mayor's job. Accordingly, the odds are from 1 to 11 to 1 to 19 in favor of the Democrats. The lone warrior is always the Republican candidate. He never fails to get his party nomination at the primaries. But he stands no more chance than a snowball in Hades on Election Day.

Of course, now and then a miracle will happen. Ex-mayor Nichols made it. Once. But not on his own power. Nor the elephant's either. He just sprawled right in on democratic roller skates. While the rest of the boys, those playful Irish youngsters were having a free-for-all. And Dan was watching it with a satanic grin. But, outside of Nichols, the only other Republican who ever sat in the mayor's chair went in in disguise. A straddle of a baby elephant, camouflaged under a donkey's skin. At the tail end of a parade made up 50-50 of Demoblicans and Repucrats with a B.L. degree from 53 State Street.

As far back as my recollection goes, His Honor, now His Excellency James Michael Curley has been the only chronic mayor Boston has ever had. He has been as unavoidable as the flu. As regular in his four-year terms as the Pharaons' seven-lean-year cycles. But nobody begrudges him his regularity. In his own rough-and-tumble way, he has been a darned sight better mayor, a more likable chap, than some of his predecessors or successors. The only bad feature about him is his permanency. If he hangs on to the governor's office as long as he did hang on to the mayor's office, he'll have the boys on Beacon Hill praying for an earthquake. For any sort of calamity that may pry him loose from the gubernatorial throne.

If School Street was famous in the old days, it is positively notorious today. On account of recent events. The glory of its ancient buildings has almost faded away. Sight-Seeing busses no longer stop before them. Not even before the City Hall. They go a little further down. Toward Washington Street, They pull up at the curb in front of a narrow doorway, between Posner's and Purcell's. At 27 School Street The Niles Building.

In fact, they don't need to go any further to get their money's worth. For the Niles Building, in its modest simplicity, has a history. A past. A past with a thrill. But a greater thrill than it can derive from it's association with the Eben D. Jordan's estate. What's the history? The past? The guide of a tourist bus will tell you. He will point to the Niles Building with reverence. Listen to him.

"This is the Niles Building, ladies and gentlemen," he will megaphone to his audience. "The baby mint which has coined more money for the New England folks than all of the national recovery acts put together. The building which has seen more real dough than the Ward System of Bakeries. The building which has given more heartaches to the boys of State Street and Federal Street than the panic of January and February 1933.

"Gaze at that building, ladies and gentlemen, for there stands before your eyes the eighth wonder of the world. The former headquarters of Charlie Ponzi, the "Wizard" of finance who made $15,000,000 in nine months out of a six-cent coupon. Just think of it, ladies and gentlemen! Fifteen millions of golden simoleons! More money than you and I can ever hope to see! Can you picture what the bambino could do for the forgotten man in these depression times with a lone thousand-dollar bill, instead of a six-cent coupon? He could pay the National debt half a dozen times, even after this administration gets through piling it up. He could pay it without batting an eye and still have more money left over than all of the Morgans, and the Rockefellers, and the Mellons and the Fords put together!"

"Take one last look, ladies and gentlemen, and let us move on. I am feeling dizzy."

What the guide may tell the tourists does not explain, however, how I happened to locate in School Street. Not that it matters in the least. But it dove-tails with the story. Especially, that, if I hadn't moved to School Street, I would have remained over the Tremont Trust Company, in Court Street. And brother Simon would have thrown one thousand and one fits at having me for a tenant.

This is what took place. It was the spring of 1919. Several months before, I had eased myself out of the job I had. Tired of working for expectations that didn't pay either my rent or my grocery bills. Tired of making money for my employers in general and none for myself.

I had a few dollars. Very few. Just enough to humor the family budget for a while. And I was undecided whether to get myself another job at $20 or $25 per, working for others, or shoot the works in a business venture of my own. But sound judgment did not prevail. I went and hired a room over the old Puritan Trust Company. An inside room.

The room had a roll-top desk and an armchair. It could have been called an office, if there had been any business attached to it. But there wasn't. All I used it for was to spend a few hours in privacy and concentration. Filling pads full of figures. Big figures. Something like Charlie Dawes' at the German Reparation Conference. Only mine dealt with dollars and cents. His with marks. Yes, easy marks.

It is hard to say whether my dollars and cents were actual. Or just mere hopes. But I know that by the time the building was taken over by the Tremont Trust Company, with an extensive plan of alterations, I had reached the conclusion that; it I was an asset to any employer, I was a greater asset to myself. Never figuring that I might be one of those assets which are spelled without the final "et". So, I took my pencils and pads, as the furniture did not belong to me, and moved into the Niles Building in School Street. There, I took possession of a dingy, little office on the fifth floor.

The necessary furniture and equipment, such as desks, chairs, typewriter, files and even a multigraph, came from installment houses. Books, directories, etc., some from my house and some from second-hand bookstores. I put in a phone. A supply of engraved stationery. And had a sign painted on the door serving notice to the world that Charles Ponzi was an exporter and importer.

That's how I happened to locate in School Street. Without premeditation. Without malice aforethought. Without any intention of snooping upon the boys across the alley from me. At the City Hall. And if from my windows I could look right into theirs, neither the Watch and Ward, nor the Finance Commission had anything to do with the arrangement. For a wonder. Because those birds haven't missed a single sure bet yet. And they have been in the habit of digging up more dirt than a steam shovel.

CHAPTER XII

MR. PONZI PROMOTES "THE TRADER'S GUIDE" WITH A 3,000,000 CIRCULATION RIGHT OFF THE BAT

When I rented the School Street office, it was my intention to become a commission agent for domestic and foreign firms. A sort of foreign department, especially for those who could not afford to maintain one of their own. And I can say that I possessed the qualifications to give satisfaction. But I had no connections. Either in the United States or abroad. So I set about to make them. Through the medium of circulars. Only to realize that between the cost of overheads, stationery and postage, they stood me from five cents for the domestic to eight cents each for the foreign circulars. Entirely too much money. At that rate, my limited resources would have faded away to nothing before I had obtained any appreciable returns.

I looked around for a less expensive way to reach my prospects. I studied the expediency of advertising. Especially in foreign trade publications. And I soon became convinced that the field was inadequately covered. The leading foreign trade publication had, at that time, a circulation of barely 50,000 copies per month. Its advertising rates were utterly out of proportion with the services it rendered. Evidently, what was needed was a new publication which could offer a greater circulation at lower rates. So, I devised such a publication. In all of its details. I called it "The Trader's Guide." And undertook its promotion under the name of "The Bostonian Advertising & Publishing Company." A long name which only meant an additional sign on the door and new letterheads.

The first problem was that of attaining a wide circulation. World-wide. Free distribution was the answer. People never refuse what does not cost them anything. It's human nature all over. But they would have no earthly use for my publication, unless they could read it. Therefore, it would have to be printed in various languages. Not in all of them. English, French, Italian, German, Spanish and Portuguese would have been enough.

The matter of mailing lists was easily solved. Directories, both domestic and foreign, the U. S. Bureau of Foreign & Domestic Commerce and the U S. Consular Service, gave me all the names I wanted. Classified in every possible way. But I couldn't undertake to mail millions of copies of each issue. The cost and the amount of work would have been prohibitive. I decided, therefore, to mail 100,000 copies every six months. And to reach each time a different set of readers. Until my mailing lists were exhausted. But it was a "Long Way to Tipperary" because I had three or more millions of names.

There is where I had to call all of my ingenuity to the rescue. In the first place, I had to keep alive the interest in the copies of The Trader's Guide already distributed. Other publications did that by publishing a new issue each month. But they covered always the same limited number of subscribers. While I had an almost unlimited number of readers to reach.

Secondly, since The Trader's Guide contained both some reading matter and some advertising of regional interest only, I had to find a way to mail into each section only what might be of local interest. For instance, an Eskimo would no more be interested in refrigerators or electric fans, than a Congo coon would be in fur coats and heating appliances.

The only way out of my difficulties was through a loose-leaf device. In fact, I picked out a cheap expansion cover with a couple of screw binder posts. I planned to mail one to each reader with only those pages of reading matter and advertising that might be of interest to him. From time to time, as new pages would be published, I intended to send them to him so that he might add them to his book. Keep it up-to-date. Each new set of 100,000 readers would receive, of course, the same cover already sent out to others and all of the pages published up to then. Such a scheme of distribution would have placed a complete and up-to-date copy of The Trader's Guide in the hands of 200,000 readers the first year, and of 200,000 new readers each year after that.

How was I going to pay for all that, if the publication was being distributed free? Easily enough. By selling advertising space. The proportion of reading matter to advertising space was 1 to 3. That is, for every page of reading matter, I would sell three pages of advertising. Could I sell it? Certainly If other publications did, there was no reason why mine shouldn't. I had more to offer than they had, for the same money. For less money in fact.

The leading publications at that time were asking - and getting - about $500 a page for advertising space. For each monthly issue. It reached only 50,000 subscribers. The Trader's Guide, for the same amount, would have placed the same ad before 100,000 readers. Not only this, but the loose-leaf feature gave the advertisers the means of reaching only the readers they wanted to reach, excluding all others.

Again, each issue of a monthly publication has only a 30-day existence. An issue is current until the next one is published. Then it becomes obsolete. It is usually thrown away. Or sold to the junk-man. To keep, therefore, the same page ad before the same 50,000 subscribers for one year, it would cost the advertiser $6,000. But The Trader's Guide, instead, never became obsolete. It was a book of permanent reference which had to be kept year after year, in order to put and classify the newly published pages under the same loose-leaf cover. Therefore, between paying $500 for a 30-day display, or the same amount for a permanent display, while reaching a number of readers twice as large, the advertisers could not hesitate. They would have given the preference to The Trader's Guide. Because my selling arguments could not be beaten. Or even matched by my competitors.

All figured, an issue of The Trader's Guide, including cover, 50 pages of reading matter, 150 pages of advertising and postage to destination, would have stood me about 35 cents a copy. Or, $35,000 for 100,000 copies. The 150 pages of advertising would have brought in over $75,000. Advertising on the cover, probably another $5,000. The net margin of profit should have been around $15,000 for the first six months. And progressively more after that.

The Trader's Guide was a good thing. I thought so. I still think so. I said so. Everybody agreed with me and said so. Yet, nobody seemed to think enough of it to help finance it.

Among others, an ex-governor of Massachusetts. He was extremely liberal with interviews. And encouragement. But tighter than a drum-head otherwise. I could not persuade him to buy half an interest in the Guide for $5,000. I suppose he would have declined even the Boston Common at $5 an acre.

I looked for money everywhere. Found it nowhere. Nevertheless, I kept up the struggle to the end. Pawned the family jewels. Mortgaged the household furniture. I didn't sell my soul to the devil, because he found he could get it for nothing if he waited long enough for it.

In a moment of despair, I decided to apply for a loan at a bank. I must have been desperate. Or I would have known better. I applied for a $2,000 loan at the Hanover Trust Company. For several months I had carried a checking account there. Really, it was more of a pain in the neck than an account. The bank thought so. I differed. Yet, every other day, I had to race to the receiving teller's window on the stroke of nine a.m. to cover some checks which I had given out after banking hours. Although I always managed to get to the bank ahead of my checks, the bookkeeper must have had an awful time to keep up with them.

When I applied for the loan, I tried to look unconcerned. I asked for 2,000 dollars with the same inflection with which I would have asked change for a nickel. My application did not get very far. It never reached the loan committee, as the bank's president heard of it, and disposed of it between a couple of puffs of his cigar. The note I offered the bank as collateral failed to impress him. So did my statement that I was a depositor in his bank.

"Sorry," he said frigidly, "but I cannot approve the loan. While it is our policy to accommodate our depositors whenever we can, your account is more of a bother than a benefit to us. Good day, Sir.'"

His last remark made me so mad that I could have spat poison. I watched him re-enter his private office. Then I left the bank muttering to myself: "Some day I'll have that bird eat out of my hand!"

A few months later the prophecy materialized. By then, I owned the Hanover Trust Company. Lock, stock and barrel. I had a $5,000,000 balance in that bank. I was only the largest stockholder, the chairman of the board of directors, and a permanent member of the executive committee.

At one of our weekly meetings, the treasurer introduced a motion to raise the president's salary. One of my men - the executive committee was just padded with them - opposed the motion. I sat there indifferently. The treasurer, peeved, suggested that the question be put to a vote. The suggestion was accepted. We voted on the basis of our stock holdings. The treasurer figured that between what he and the president owned and the proxies they held, plus the stray independent votes, they would carry the motion. But I owned 1,625 shares and controlled, by agreement, 600 more. Out of a total issue of 4,000 shares. My vote was "no."

"I am licked!" said the president after the votes were counted.

"Of course, you are!" I told him. "You licked yourself when you refused me a $2,000 loan about six months ago. Do you remember?"

"Probably not. But I have not forgotten," I went on. "You told me then that my account was more of a bother than a benefit to this bank. Because it was small. Perhaps, it was a bother. But you showed a deplorable lack of tact for a bank president. That small account shows today a $5,000,000 balance. More than all of the other deposits put together. After your remark of six months ago, I would have been justified in closing my account. And this bank would not have me today as a depositor. Today I am refusing you a raise because I don't believe you are much of an asset to this bank.

"Then, there is nothing else for me to do, but hand in my resignation," he said.

"Your resignation?" I retorted. "You can do as you please about that. But I don't see where you, are in a position to resign. I own this bank. You are one of my employees. Just now, you can keep on as President. If I should at any time decide that I don't want you around, I'll fire you."

But, after this digression, let me resume the narrative. Back in my office - which, by the way had been moved to larger quarters on the second floor - from my call at the Hanover Trust, I summoned my help. Two stenographers and a boy. I informed them that their services would no longer be required after the coming Saturday. Because I could not pay their wages. They offered to remain. To work for "expectations". I could not and did not consent to it. But I was deeply touched by their loyalty.

My next step was to insert a small ad in the papers. Desk space to sublet, or something to that effect. This brought some immediate results. In less than a week I had several tenants. My rent money was taken care of. The glass door which formerly read: "Charles Ponzi, Export & Import" and "The Bostonian Adv. & Publ. Co.," with the addition of new names, began to look like a directory. My dignity, perhaps, suffered somewhat. But what I lost in dignity, I gained in peace of mind.

I dismissed The Trader's Guide from my mind. Another house of cards had collapsed. That did not matter. I was getting accustomed to chasing rainbows. As one would, fade away, I would pursue another. For a dreamer, I certainly was persevering. I never was a quitter. Undaunted by failure, I transferred my attention from The Trader's Guide to international reply coupons. A new rainbow had come within my range of vision. The most spectacular I ever saw. With renewed energy and enthusiasm, I chased after it. I caught up with it. When I did, I found fifteen millions of dollars at the end of it. I should have called it a day. And quitted while - the quitting was good. I didn't. Hence, this story.

CHAPTER XIII

MR. PONZI FINALLY DISCOVERS AN UNTRODDEN PATH TO FABULOUS WEALTH AND TAKES IT

The "racket" of international reply coupons actually fell in my lap like a ripe apple. I did not have to shake the tree to get it. I just reached over, where it had fallen, and took it. It looked good. Luscious. I examined it for flaws. Found none. I had to bite. I wouldn't have been human if I didn't.

Sorting my correspondence, I noticed a letter from Spain. It had an international reply coupon pinned to the corner. The letter had been on my desk for several days. I read it. It did not say much. It merely asked for a copy of The Trader's Guide. And the coupon had been enclosed in prepayment of postage. I had seen and used coupons before. I knew what they were. I knew their exact function.

The coupon before me was identical in appearance to others I had handled before. It had been issued by a Spanish post office. But corresponded in every detail with the coupons issued by other countries. The only minor difference was that, at the bottom, it had the word "Espana" (Spain), instead of the name of some other country. Likewise, at the top, the value appeared in Spanish and read: "30 centavos".

The main legend appeared on the face and the reverse of the coupon in several languages. It said: "This coupon may be exchanged at any post-office of any country in the Universal Postal Union for a postage stamp of the value of 25 centimes, or its equivalent."

The coupon came to my notice accidentally. At a time when my mind was extremely alert. But it was entirely due to what I already knew about coupons and foreign exchange rates that I saw in it an opportunity for speculation. An untrodden shortcut to some easy money. And it may seem strange, almost amazing, that my path to some easy money might have been overlooked until then by the financial wizards of Wall Street. But it happened. And those birds have never forgiven me since. For having caught them napping. Whenever you steal a march on them, you can bet your bottom dollar that they are going to be on your trail until your beneficiary collects on your insurance policy.

My discovery didn't involve much scientific study. In fact it did not involve either science or study. It was a good deal simpler, than the Einstein theory of relativity. So simple, really, that it took me less than five minutes of figuring on a scratch pad to realize its possibilities.

The coupon itself told a brief story. It had been purchased at a Spanish post-office for 30 centavos. Nominally equivalent to 6 cents United States. It could be exchanged, in the United States, for a postage stamp of a denomination equivalent to 25 centimes, or 5 cents. It remained to be ascertained whether the coupon could actually be exchanged in the United States. A call at the Boston post-office would have settled that question in no time. But there was no hurry for it.

What set me thinking was the knowledge that the peseta - the Spanish monetary unit - was then quoted 15 cents in American money, instead of 20 cents, its par value. A little figuring disclosed that, at that rate, six and two-thirds pesetas could be bought for one dollar. Since a peseta was made up of 100 centavos, six and two-thirds pesetas were equal to 666 centavos. It didn't take much to find out that with 666 centavos, I could have bought at any Spanish post-office 22 coupons exactly like the one before me. Coupons which I could exchange in the United States for a 5 cent stamp each. Or, $1.10. The transaction showed a 10% profit.

A 10% margin wasn't much of a speculation. But one thought led to another. Some foreign currencies had suffered even a greater depreciation than the peseta. The Italian lira, for instance. It was quoted then about 5 cents instead of 20 cents. One lira was equal to 100 centesimi. A dollar would have brought 20 lire, or 2,000 centesimi. With 2,000 centesimi I could have obtained 66 coupons at 30 centesimi each. Or enough coupons to obtain in exchange for them at the Boston post-office $3.30 of 5-cent stamps. A gross profit of 230%.

Just then I was dealing only with theories. In my own heart, I felt sure of my figures and conclusions. Had I owned as little as a few hundred dollars, I would not have hesitated to play a lone hand. My financial circumstances made it impossible. As usual. When I had a good thing I could never swing it alone. Faced with the necessity of borrowing from others, I found that I needed something more substantial than my own theories and beliefs. I could not approach any prospective lender until I possessed unimpeachable evidence that my assertions were absolutely accurate.

First of all, it was important to ascertain whether the depreciation of paper currencies had in any way affected the selling cost of the coupons. To this end, I sent out three letters. Each with a dollar bill enclosed. One went to Spain, one to France and the third one to Italy. In each case, I requested the recipient to exchange the dollar bill into paper currency of his own country. Then to purchase with it as many coupons as he could obtain and mail them to me. In the course of a few weeks, I received the replies and the coupons. The results coincided with my expectations.

In the meanwhile, inquiry at the Boston post-office had satisfied me that the coupons have been exchanged there without trouble.

A copy of the United States Postal Guide and any newspaper with current quotations on foreign exchange completed the chain of evidence necessary to support ray statements. In all, it had cost me less than four dollars to lay the foundation of a venture which nine months thence, had an outstanding indebtedness of $15,000,000.

The peculiar feature about the whole thing was that the laws and the treaties involved in the purchase and redemption of coupons protected the user of such coupons and not the various governments concerned. They could not refuse either to sell or to redeem the coupons without adequate advance notice. Even though they might be aware of the fact that a speculation in them was in progress. And that they stood to lose money by it.

The coupons were a commodity like postage stamps. They were a part and parcel of that postal service which, being a government monopoly; the government guaranteed and had to perform satisfactorily. Regardless of whether it showed a profit or a deficit. The post-offices of any country could refuse to sell me stamps. They could not limit the number of coupons I wanted either to buy or redeem. They could not decline to increase their normal supply, if it became necessary to meet an increased demand. In other words, the burden of living up to the terms of the contract was entirely on the government's side and not on mine. All I could be expected to do was to tender cash in payment of coupons.

Coupons in exchange for stamps. But what I did with the stamps afterwards, was nobody else's business but my own.

There was no law or rule or regulation I could possibly violate by traffic in coupons, carried on as described here. The most that could be said was that such traffic might have been unethical. But a breach of ethics was not an infraction of the law. Anyway, environment had made me rather callous on the subject of ethics. Then, as now, nobody gave a rap for ethics. The almighty dollar was the only goal. And its possession placed a person beyond criticism for any breach of ethics incidental to the acquisition of it.

My early attempts to borrow substantial sums failed utterly. People wanted to know too much about my plans. More than was safe to tell. Had I been too liberal with information, somebody might have used it himself. And left me out in the cold. So I told just enough to whet the people's greed and curiosity. No more.

I wasted very little time and effort in my quest for capital in lump sums. I soon gave it up as a bad job. Because I knew I could borrow ten dollars each from ten different persons much easier than I could borrow one hundred dollars from one. But in order to borrow even small amounts from strangers, I realized that I needed a certain prestige. Such as a firm name lends. Because it has the appearance of greater stability. And so, I decided to form a company. And I adopted for it the name of the Securities Exchange Company. Convinced that I was on the right track, I was determined to see the thing through to the end. And didn't I though! But what a different end than I had anticipated!

CHAPTER XIV

MR. PONZI ORGANIZES THE SECURITIES EXCHANGE COMPANY ON THE PATTERN OF A ONE-MAN-BAND

The organization of the Securities Exchange Company was a very simple matter. In those days, there were no blue-sky laws to contend with. Not in Massachusetts, at any rate. Because the so-called Securities Act was not enacted until 1921. Which, by the way, insofar as I was concerned, was like locking the stable after the horse had been stolen.

Simple as it was, the matter of organization presented a few minor problems. A corporate form was out of the question I did not know how to draw up the articles of incorporation. I did not care to take the usual run of lawyers into my confidence. Those I might trust, I couldn't afford. Those I might afford, I couldn't trust. Then, the incidental cost of incorporation was more than I cared to incur.

Since I had decided not to operate under my own name, a partnership was the only alternative. After a little study of the situation, I found it inadequate. Desirable partners were beyond my reach. Undesirable ones, I did not want. There was nothing left for me to do, but to devise some new form of organization. Something that would fill the bill and cost no money. A "partnerless" partnership was the outcome.

The legal status of such a partnership may be a debatable question. However, that point was never raised during the litigation that followed the collapse of my venture. The Securities Exchange Company was treated as a "one-man company." Evidently, it must be technically possible at law for a man "to keep company with himself." Honestly, there are more freaks at law than in a dime museum! And they are not all on the bench, either.

When an obliging clerk at the Boston City Hall furnished me with the necessary registration blank, I discovered that I was required to fill in the names of the various members of my company. I put myself down as manager. So as to gain time. And do some quick thinking. Had I hesitated, what would the clerk have thought?

The name of John S. Dondero came to my mind. He was my uncle by marriage. A reputable man. The registration was only a formality, after all. I did not anticipate any consequence. So, I put him down as one of the partners. Confident that he would never know. If he did, I could explain the unauthorized use of his name.

The second name which occurred to me was that of a man I had known in Italy. A man I thought dead. But it developed later that the report of his demise had been "slightly exaggerated". Like Mark Twain's death. He was very much alive. Not knowing that, I put his name down with a chuckle. He, at least, would never know or care!

That was my conception of a "partnerless" partnership. A most ideal form of organization. Silent. Unobtrusive. Yet sufficient to cover the law. Had I known then what was to come, I would have made it still more ideal. By putting another dead man in my uncle's place. That would have saved him a lot of undeserved trouble. And given me even greater security. Dead men cause no dissension. Neither are they reached by court writs. Nor cited for contempt.

The Securities Exchange Company began its business career under the most favorable auspices. True, it had no capital. But it had no black eye either. And no liabilities. For a wonder. The total cost of organization had set me back a trifle. Only about the price of three and one-third packages of cigarettes. I smoked Murads then. At fifteen cents a package everywhere. Flat. Except at the United Cigar Stores. There, you got the cigarettes and a coupon for the same price.

After the registration, my company was officially existent. But that was about all. It had an address. Some furniture and equipment. But no letter-heads and other essential stationery. I still needed about 50 bucks to be actually ready for business. With a budget showing a steady deficit, like the national budget. I could not have saved fifty dollars in fifty months. In fact, I couldn't have lasted that long, anyway.

Things looked bad. It seemed as if there were no fifty dollars in the whole of Boston. Except, perhaps in some of the big banks where they generally have on hand at least fifty bucks. To make matters worse, some of my creditors began to pester me for installments due, past due and over-due. I couldn't plug a hole fast enough that another one would spring a leak. It was the most diuretic situation I ever met with.

One of the creditors made his appearance quite regularly. He was a furniture dealer from the North End. His specialty - everything in household goods for newlyweds. From non-squeaking bed-springs to rolling pins. I owed him for my office furniture. Some white-pine desks and chairs they had palmed off on me for quartered oak.

He was in an ugly mood when he called that day. But for his size, he might have looked dangerous. Since he was only a little runt, like me, I didn't get alarmed. I invited him to sit down and he hesitated.

"For the love of Mike, sit down!" I urged him. "That chair is still yours and won't place you under any obligations."

He sat down and started to pull some papers out of his pocket. Mortgage, bills, receipts, and so forth. I waived the presentation of the evidence. None was necessary to remind me of what I couldn't forget. Namely, what I owed him.

He was determined to get some money out of me that day. Either that or the furniture. The money was not worrying me. I did not have it and that settled it and he couldn't draw blood out of a turnip. But I didn't want to lose the furniture. The idea of having to sit on the windowsill, did not appeal to me at all. I am sort of funny that way.

I had to capitulate. Having no cash, I offered him the next best thing to it. A promissory note.

"Of what good is your note to me? he asked with a certain inflection of contempt. "I have your mortgage note now."

"I know you have," I told him, "but this is something else. Listen," I kept on trying to be convincing, "I am going to make you a proposition, but first you must answer me a few questions. You have a bank account, of course?"

"I have," he admitted.

"Is your credit standing at the bank good enough so that you can discount some notes now and then?"

"It is," he answered.

"Would you have any trouble in discounting, let us say. a 200 dollar note?" was my next question.

"No I don't think so," he said.

"Well, now," I insisted, "if I should give you a 60-day note for 200 dollars, you could take it to the bank and get your money on it, couldn't you?"

"I could," he acknowledged.

"All right. Now then, if you could apply that money, or any part of it, to the payment of my bill, it wouldn't make a particle of difference to you where the money came from, would it?" I pressed on.

"No. Of course, not. So long as the note was paid at maturity," he conceded.

"Exactly. Now, my proposition is this," I stated. "I will give you a 60-day note for $200. You will discount it at your bank and credit my account for $100. The balance you will hold at my disposal. I will draw against it as I need."

"You will have to show me first how you are going to take that note up at maturity," he said.

"Certainly," I agreed. "I shall do that right now."

For the next fifteen minutes I talked to him on international reply coupons. I gave him the whole history. From the treaty of Rome in 1907 to date. I showed him a coupon. Told him to keep it and try to exchange it at the post-office. I made him read the United States Official Postal Guide at page 37. Then I explained to him the market quotations on foreign exchange. In other words, I gave him the works. And when I got through, he was entirely sold on the proposition. He accepted the note.

Incidentally, my only agreement with him was to redeem that note at maturity with the usual interest I kept my part of the agreement. Not only had I redeemed that note, but I also settled his bill in full. And dismissed the matter from my mind.

Five months later, out of a clear sky, I found myself the defendant in a million dollar suit brought by the same fellow. On the strength of that promissory note, he claimed a half interest in the Securities Exchange Company. He sued. And it cost me $50,000 to get out of it. But, more of this later.

With sufficient money for the printing of stationery and other minor expenses, I completed my plan of operation. I decided to borrow money from the public at large. In amounts from $10 up. Against the promissory notes of the Securities Exchange Company. The proceeds were to be used in the purchase of coupons. The notes were to be payable in 90 days and carry a 50% interest. Actually, I adopted the practice of taking up my notes at 45 days from date. Thus paying interest at the rate of 400% a year.

The moment I found myself equipped for business, I began to look for investors. Calling here and there. Talking about my company. Its notes. The coupons. But never really soliciting investments. I knew that curiosity would eventually lead to further inquiry and to my office.

In fact, one day I had a caller. My first caller. He had heard about my proposition and wanted to know more about it. I told him all there was to know.

I can't say that he was convinced by my representations. He understood the thing, all right. But he appeared more impressed by the 50% feature than by the technique of my plan. Evidently, he was no "connoisseur," of art. I could see from the expression of his face that he was doing some mental figuring. Probably, pyramiding some imaginary investment. Whatever passed through his mind, left him enough caution to resist temptation. He did not invest. Said he could not afford it.

The realization that I was about to lose my first sale and, with it, probably a certain amount of confidence in myself, urged me to offer him an agency. It was a brand new idea. The result of impulse. Rather than of sober consideration. But impulse and nerve constituted then about nine-tenths of my assets.

When I told him that, by explaining my proposition to his friends, he could earn a ten-per-cent commission on whatever money they might invest, he accepted the agency. I gave him no credentials. He needed none. But I gave him a one-lesson course in salesmanship and psychology. He needed that. Especially in view of my new ideas on the subject.

I had a good thing. There was no doubt in my mind about that. Being a good thing, it needed no high-pressure salesmanship. No unnecessary stress upon its advantages. I was selling my dollars at about 66 cents. That's all there was to it. And they were good dollars. Any attempt to force them upon a prospective investor would have been to create suspicion, rather than confidence. Therefore, I told him that, in order to be successful, he should never crowd a prospect. Never go beyond the mere details of the coupon transaction. Once those were grasped, people could not fail to invest.

And they didn't fail. Later events proved that I was right. That I knew human nature. That I was a better salesman by instinct than others by training. In those days, any proposition connected with foreign exchange was more popular than a gold mine. I counted upon that to obtain attention. To give me an opening for further details. The 50% feature would have done the rest. It would have struck a responsive chord in the heart of every man and woman. As it did. Because we are all gamblers. We all crave easy money. And plenty of it. If we didn't, no get-rich-quick scheme could be successful.

My proposition was decidedly tempting. Apparently, fool proof. It could be tested with a ten-dollar bill. It might have looked economically unsound as an investment. But it was extremely attractive as a gamble.

People gambled with me as I thought they would. They gave me ten dollars as a lark. When they received fifteen at the end of 45 days, all sense of caution left them. They plunged in for all they were worth. They brought their friends along. The legion of my investors grew by leaps and bounds. Each satisfied customer became a self-appointed sales man. It was their combined salesmanship, and not my own, that put the thing over. I admit that I started a small snowball down hill. But it developed into an avalanche by itself.

My first salesman was the snowball. Up to January 1, 1920, he rounded up exactly 18 investors. For a total amount of $1,770. The snowball had started on its way down hill. It gained momentum when, about the second week in February I paid to my early investors $2,478 on their original investment of $1,770. From then on, the number of investors grew rapidly, and steadily. By the end of July, they were exactly 30,219. They held notes of the Securities Exchange Company for nearly $15,000,000. The snowball had attained the proportions of an avalanche. Which might have traveled much further before striking bottom. But for my own excess of confidence in men and fate. And caused a different story to be written.

The Rise Of Mr. Ponzi

Headlines like this one, published in *The Boston Post,* during the summer of 1920, helped bring about the collapse of Ponzi's investment scheme. In this issue of the paper it is reported that Charles Ponzi, *aka* Charles Ponsi, *aka* Charles Bianchi, had served prison time in Canada for the offense of forgery.

Charles Ponzi

Charles Ponzi, August 1920, working at his desk at the offices of the Securities Exchange Company at 27 School Street, Boston, Massachusetts. Ponzi appears to be signing a promissory note. He promised investors a 50% return in 45 days or 100% return if investments were allowed to mature for 90 days.

The Rise Of Mr. Ponzi

Ponzi raked in over $10 million dollars in about six months through his investment scheme involving international postal reply coupons. Here he is playing the part of the respected, well dressed and confident businessman. Ponzi always dressed immaculately in tailored business suits, sported a gold handled walking stick and wore a large diamond stick pin in his neck tie.

Charles Ponzi, the 'Pied Piper of Boston,' leading some of his many followers to the local courthouse in August 1920. Although Ponzi was subsequently convicted of mail fraud and ordered to prison, some investors continued to mail him money so he could invest it for them after his release from jail.

The Rise Of Mr. Ponzi

Another shot of the man who perfected the 'rob Peter to pay Paul' investment pyramid scheme. Notice the confidence Ponzi exudes. Thousands of gullible investors were duped into believing Ponzi could make them wealthy through his get-rich-quick scheme! Today, the Ponzi scheme is still used by swindlers to defraud unsuspecting victims of their money.

Charles Ponzi

Charles Ponzi surrounded by law enforcement officials after his arrest in Texas after trying to flee to Italy. He is being escorted back to Boston to begin a stint in a Massachusetts state prison.

The Rise Of Mr. Ponzi

Charles Ponzi waves goodbye to photographers as he walks up the gang plank of the S.S. Vulcania. He was deported back to Italy from America after his parole from prison in 1934. A few of his last words to reporters were, "I bear no grudges, I hope the world forgives me." Ponzi lived out the remainder of his life in Italy and Brazil. He died a pauper in a charity ward in Rio De Jeneiro in 1949.

CHAPTER XV

MR. PONZI'S LIFE BECOMES ONE NIGHTMARE OF POLICE AND POSTAL INSPECTORS.

The first salesman missed his vocation in life when he became a storekeeper. He should have been a missionary. He certainly could spread the gospel! His activities cannot be measured by his success. They can, by their effect. Within a week, his propaganda had reached the keen ears of one of Boston's business guardians. And I was honored by the official call of one of its representatives.

He was, a bespectacled gentleman. Of that indefinite age between senility and dotage. Such as might be expected from such an ancient institution. That's Boston all over, bless its heart! Within a radius of half a mile from the Custom House Tower, you can run across more mummies at large than you find walled in King Tut's Tomb.

My caller wasted no precious moments in idle conversation. He came right to the point. He said that the institution he represented was very much disturbed. Over the discovery that I was offering a 40 or 50 per cent return in 90 days to my investors. The illustrious remains of the Pilgrim forefathers, he stated, were getting restless in their graves. I believe he said "graves." Maybe, it was "gravies." At any rate, it was natural for them to get restless. Like the old 4% foggies in State Street.

I flashed my most disarming smile on the old gent. And set about to show him that the world, after all, had made some progress in three centuries. I exhibited to his gaze an international reply coupon. Explained to him what it was. He inspected closely. For any picture of General Lee or "Stonewall" Jackson. He found none. And heaved a sigh of relief. He was satisfied that the coupon, at least, was not a piece of confederate wallpaper.

When I told him the coupon was a product of the Universal Postal Union, he was puzzled. He did not know whether the Postal Union was a merger of the Postal Telegraph and of the Western Union. Or just a member of the American Federation of Labor. I came to his rescue. And told him all about the International Postal Congress of Rome in 1907. He was still a little skeptical. Until I opened up the United States Official Postal Guide at page 37. Then he stood up and saluted. As he would at the strains of the Star Spangled Banner.

Once he was convinced "beyond a reasonable doubt" that my wares were guaranteed by the Great Seal of the United States (or, was it that of Great Britain that impressed him most?), it was an easy matter to acquaint him with the delightful mysteries of foreign exchange. His beaming countenance followed me all the way up into the realms of seven figures. Until he almost sprouted wings. I left him there. With his head above the clouds. Gazing at a universe of eternal sunshine!

The institution he represented never disturbed my peace of mind since. In fact, I believe I became later an "honorary" member thereof. Upon the payment of a $200 admission fee. It's always an honor to be touched by them for the price of a membership. But where that institution's investigations stopped, others started.

In no time, I had a speaking acquaintance with every police and postal inspector in Boston. At the height of my career, there were more inspectors working for me than for the city, and cops too. I had so many of them around, that my office looked like police headquarters at roll call.

In fact, if headquarters were not moved earlier from Pemberton Square to Berkeley Street, I have a suspicion it was on my account. The new location would never do. Both Commissioner Curtis and Superintendent Crowley knew they couldn't even get a quorum up there. It was too far from School Street. They probably felt that the logical thing to do was to move the sign from Pemberton Square down to School Street and plank it over my office. It would have been cheaper.

It must not be assumed from what I say that I actually invited advances from the police. I am not that kind of a person. The advances were forced upon me. But I was too polite to turn them down. To resent them. I just flirted back, so to speak. Like the man who flirts with death. Because he knows he can't duck it.

In fact, one afternoon, as I was leaning backwards in my swivel chair, with my feet propped against the radiator, the phone rang. I reached over for the instrument and was greeted by a familiar voice.

"Charlie," it said. "There is a warrant out for your arrest." Just like that!

Whatever else it said, did not and does not matter. That one sentence was enough to bring my feet down from the radiator. A threat of arrest is always a shock. A man may look at himself in the mirror in the morning. And discover that he has developed small pox over night. He may take that philosophically. But let the same man know that he is about to be arrested and his first impulse will be to chase around in circles. Looking for a hiding place.

That tip over the phone actually disturbed me. There was a perfectly good supper at home in danger of going to waste. And I didn't even know what the bill-of-fare at the Charles Street jail called for. For a moment I was on the verge of calling up Sheriff Kelliher and asking him. Tell him to keep it sort of warm. But other thoughts came to my mind. Was I going to sit in my office and wait for the warrant to be served, or what? No. I decided I would not wait.

I put on my hat and coat and walked over to Pemberton Square. To Police Headquarters. I inquired about the "warrant." And was directed to the basement. I was not surprised. I had been in department stores before. And knew my geography. Probably, I thought, they were running a bargain sale in warrants. And I might get one marked down.

Below, I walked over to the warrant "counter." Perhaps, it was a desk. The "saleslady" in charge was ... a cop. For a wonder, he was almost polite. He asked me what I wanted.

"I have come for a warrant," I told him.

"All right," he said. "Let's hear the complaint. Who is the party you want to have arrested?"

"I don't want to have anybody arrested," I started to explain.

"Then, what in hell do you want?" he asked working up a temper.

"A warrant that you are supposed to have against me," I stated.

"Do you mean to say that you have come to accept service of it?" he inquired with astonishment. "That you want to, surrender?"

"Well, something like that," I admitted. "What's the use of putting you to a lot of trouble looking for me when it's just as easy for me to come over here?"

"I don't know what it's all about," he confessed, "but you certainly deserve to be commended for your attitude. Let's see, what is your name?"

"Charles Ponzi," I replied.

"How do you spell the last name?" he asked.

"P-o-n-z-i," I spelled for him.

He scanned through a big book, the blotter, until he came to the proper entry. Then he informed me that there was no warrant.

"We have been asked to look you up," he said, "and your coming here, of your own free will, is a point in your favor. Do you mind hanging around until I locate the inspector who has charge of the case?"

"No; go ahead," I said good-naturedly. Knowing there was no warrant, I felt good-natured.

Within a few minutes, I was introduced to an inspector. With him was one Joseph Merenda. I forgot in what capacity the latter was there. Probably, as an interpreter. But he was not needed. He, the inspector, and myself walked over to a desk and sat down. It developed that the police department had heard of the 50 per cent racket. And were interested. They would be.

The inspector was rather uncertain in his knowledge of postal matters. And of foreign exchange. To him too it had to be explained that the Universal Postal Union was not a "Local." Like the Hod Carriers'. And that the coupons were not clippings from Liberty Bonds. But I found him positively prejudiced against foreign exchange. Just because it was "foreign." He couldn't get through his noodle why it had not been included in the exclusion clauses of the immigration laws. Ten or more years later, I couldn't get it through my noodle either. In some instance, on which the ink isn't dry yet.

All together, the inspector was well impressed by the general outline of my plan. He pronounced it legitimate, (subject to further corroboration by the postal authorities.) On many points it appeared to him as clear as mud. But on all of the others he did not understand, he was thoroughly in accord with me.

In the meanwhile, since New Year's Day, my salesman had become scarcer than Orangemen at a St. Patrick's Day parade in South Boston.

He didn't come near me. He hadn't sent me any investors. He hadn't even called me up.

Now, I know that he was ducking. And why. After causing a few friends to invest, he felt it might be wise to keep out of sight until the payments materialized. If they didn't he would have a better start. I can't blame him for wanting to be a few lengths ahead, in the event of a race.

In fact, I was not entirely at ease myself. I had given the money to buy coupons to a friend who was working on board a transatlantic liner. I did not fear an act of dishonesty on his part but I was afraid something might happen to him. He could have been taken sick. He might have jumped overboard. Or met with an accident. That would have been just "two" bad. Yes: he and I.

With the lapsing of each day, my suspense grew keener. Until I was greeted by his unheralded appearance around the first week in February. The story he told me was gratifying. The coupons were obtainable everywhere. Even the smallest post-office carried a reasonable supply. With sufficient notice they could be procured in larger quantities. Official co-operation could be had. Through the wise distribution of small gratuities. What music could have been sweeter to my ears?

With enthusiasm, I set about to effect my first payments. I got as much thrill out of each note redeemed, as a high school girl gets out of her first kiss. It didn't matter that each of my investors drew his money out. I knew they would either come back, or send their friends. Did they? Of course, they did. They began to show up within a week or two. And up to the last of the month, they left exactly $5,290 for another spin of the wheel. I spun it for them.

CHAPTER XVI

MR. PONZI DISPROVES THE THEORY THAT THERE CANNOT BE A PROFIT WITHOUT A CORRESPONDING LOSS.

My receipts had reached the $1,000 per day mark. My friend was on his way back to Europe. And everything was going along smoothly. When somebody threw a monkey-wrench into the works.

The trouble started down the North End. I had given a couple of coupons to an Italian prospect. And told him to experiment with them at the post-office. They were United States coupons. He took them to the sub-station at the corner of Hanover and North Bennett Streets. Presented them for exchange. The man in charge refused to accept them. The Italian came back to me convinced that I trying to gyp him.

The situation called for action. Not diplomacy. My reputation was at stake. I could not afford to ignore the incident. So I reached for the phone and called the postmaster in my client's presence. Since I talked principally for the latter's benefit, I tried to be impressive. More so than considerate.

The postmaster's argument was that a reply coupon issued in the United States could be redeemed only in a foreign country. My argument was that, no matter where issued, a coupon could be redeemed at the post-office of any country belonging to the Universal Postal Union. Including the one of issue. Nothing short than a bulletin from the Third Assistant Postmaster General could have convinced that man. Our conversation did not settle the question. But the Italian was satisfied that I must have been right. Or I wouldn't have talked the way I did.

The incident was not closed by the hanging of the receiver. I dismissed it from my mind. But that postmaster didn't. He reported the matter to his superiors. And. I received an unexpected call.

I was in my private office talking to a prospect when the call came. My uncle Dondero and my wife were in the anteroom, waiting for me to get through. The tramping of "flat feet" warned me of the approach of my callers. I don't know whether they entered the anteroom with thumbs in the armholes of their vests. So as to exhibit their badges. Very likely they did. I could not see them from where I was sitting. But I heard them.

"We want to see Mr. Ponzi," one of them said in an arrogant voice.

My uncle's face, blanched by fear, appeared at the door of my private office. The poor man was scared stiff. He said, in Italian, that there were three inspectors to see me. He would not have been more awed if he had announced the Father, the Son and the Holy Ghost.

"Tell them to wait," I told him. "I am busy with this gentlemen now. I'll see them when I get through."

My uncle looked at me in amazement. He could not grasp the effrontery of anyone telling a cop to wait. He was so darned law abiding himself that he looked upon a cop as he would upon Frederick the Great in full regalia.

The fact is that I didn't mean exactly to be disdainful. But I knew the cops. It's a second nature with them to be gruffy. They like to assert authority. Their favorite method is to try intimidation first. If they can get away with it. Failing in that, they retrench and try subtlety.

I kept the officers waiting for several minutes. I did that to collect my thoughts, more than anything else. I knew the next interview was going to tax my wits. And I wanted to be prepared for it.

I escorted my caller to the door when he left. As soon as he was gone, I turned to the three officers and asked them who they were. And what they wanted. The questions were not really necessary. One of them was the inspector whom I had met before. He spoke for the others.

"I am inspector from Police Headquarters," he said. "We have come to question you."

"Oh, I see," I remarked. "You are paying me an official visit. In that case, show me your warrant."

"We have no warrant," interposed the postal inspector. "We did not come to make an arrest. Just to ask you some questions."

"In that case," I observed, "you must be aware of the fact that you are on my premises entirely at my own tolerance. I don't have to answer any of your questions, unless I want to."

"But you would not refuse to answer our questions?" he asked.

"Wouldn't I? I certainly would," I informed him. "You cannot assume an attitude of proprietorship around my office and get away with it. You may take me in custody. With a proper warrant. And I will not resist. But, without it, I have a right to resent your presence here."

The postal inspector must have realized that I could not be intimidated. He changed tactics. He acknowledged my rights in the matter. But suggested that a brief conference, in a friendly spirit, might prove advantageous all around. I agreed with him. And invited them into my private office.

The conversation opened up like a fencing bout. With a series of feints and parries. Apparently, the inspectors wanted my version of the argument with the postmaster of the Hanover Street sub-station. Actually, they didn't give a rap about that. What they were after, was evidence of fraud in my reported activities in coupons. But I was on my guard. And declined to be led into any admission of fact.

"I believe we are wasting a lot of precious time," I urged. "This postmaster's report of his alleged conversation with me is not evidence that the conversation itself occurred. If it did occur and you have reason to believe it constituted a violation of the law on my part, bring charges and the matter will be thrashed out in court. But it is extremely naive of you to come to me for any statement which you hope to use against me."

"We are not contemplating any action against you, Mr. Ponzi," answered the postal inspector. "But we are interested in some of the things you told that postmaster."

"Just a moment inspector," I interrupted. "You mean that you are interested in some of the statements "attributed" to me by that postmaster. There is no evidence that I ever said anything to him."

"Oh, all right," he conceded shrugging his shoulders, "have it your own way. I suppose you will not admit knowing any thing about international reply coupons either?"

"You are wrong again, inspector," I said. "I have no objection in telling you whatever little I know about coupons. If it can be of any help to you."

Right there, we launched into an extensive discussion of that particular subject. We analyzed it from every angle. And finally agreed upon the theory that a profitable speculation in coupons was possible. The inspector, however, was of the opinion that a large number of coupons could not be either bought or redeemed.

"I differ with you, Mr. Inspector," I said. "You know that there is no limit to the number of stamps a person can buy from the government. Well, then," I went on after he had agreed with me on that point, "do you know of any good reason why a person should not be able to buy any number of coupons?"

He did not know of any reason. Nor did he know why any number of them couldn't be redeemed, if one could.

"They may be counterfeits," he suggested.

"We are not discussing that kind of coupons, inspector," I remarked. "We are talking about coupons which are genuine beyond all doubts."

"Well," he insisted, "the government may decline to redeem them."

"No," I stated. "The government cannot do that. Not so long as it is a party to the international postal treaty."

"I don't know a thing about international law," he confessed.

"Neither do I," I said, "but I use common sense and reach my own conclusions."

"You seem to know a whole lot more than I gave you credit for at first," he blurted out.

"Now, don't make me blush, Mr. Inspector," I pleaded. "Really, I don't know enough to get out of the rain."

The inspector did not consider himself check-mated yet. He argued that if a speculation in coupons resulted in a profit for someone, it must result in a loss for someone else.

"If it does, I have been unable to discover who is the loser." I told him. "In fact, I am inclined to believe that everybody makes a profit."

"That's absurd!" the inspector contended.

"And so is a giraffe," I retorted in my own fresh way.

"Do yon remember the story about the old rube who had never seen one? When one was shown him, he said; "There ain't no such animal!" "Now, inspector, if you don't mind, I am going to show you a giraffe."

This is the way I put it up to him: "Let us assume," I said, "that France needs fifteen millions of francs. I borrow in this country one million dollars at 50% interest, as I am doing now on a small scale. The million dollars, at the current rate of exchange, is equal to fifteen millions of francs. I send a draft for it to the French government with the understanding that France will issue to me 50,000,000 of international reply coupons. France can obtain the coupons from the Universal Postal Union on open account. As soon as I receive the coupons, I exchange them here for stamps. Then I sell the stamps at 10% discount. Let us assume that I pay also a 10% commission to the agents who have been instrumental in obtaining for me one million dollars from the public. The transaction, in so far as I am concerned, would show the following balance:

Cash on hand from sale of 50,000,000 U.S. 5¢ stamps (less 10% discount)	$2,250,000.00
Principal due to note holders	$1,000,000.00
50% interest	$ 500,000.00
10% commission to agents	$ 100,000.00
Gross profit for myself	$ 650,000.00
	$2,250,000.00

"On the other hand, the ledger of the Universal Postal Union would show the United States government a creditor to the extent of $2,500,000 and the French government a debtor to the extent of $3,000,000. Why three million dollars? Because the coupons cost the French government 15,000,000 Francs payable in gold, at their gold parity of 5 francs to the dollar. While they didn't cost me but one million dollars, at the current exchange rate of 15 francs to the dollar. The difference between what France must pay and what the United States can collect, represents the charges of the Universal Postal Union for the service.

"I will now assume that France is called upon to settle that indebt edness. Since it has received only one million dollars and owes three millions, it faces a loss of $2,000,000. The loss cannot be avoided so long as the franc remains at the ratio of 15 to the dollar. But, if that ratio should decrease, the loss would decrease in proportion. It would entirely disappear if, and when, the franc sold at its gold parity of 5 to the dollar. However, as a general rule, depreciated currencies require a number of years to recover.

"The settlement with the Universal Postal Union cannot be deferred by France. The payment must be effected. And the best way is to finance it through a bond issue. An issue of $3,000,000 of twenty-year 3% bonds, payable in dollars. The carrying charges for the bonds will amount to $1,800,000 in twenty years."

"But it must be remembered that France has already on hand 15,000,000 francs derived from the sale of the coupons to me. The 15,000,000 francs, if loaned by the French government to private or public self-liquidating enterprises, for a period of twenty years, and at an annual interest of 5%, would in twenty years, amount to 30,000,000 francs and would then be equal to 6,000,000 dollars. They would be sufficient to retire the bond issue, with interest charges of $1,800,000, and, in addition, leave a profit of $1,200,000 for the French government.

"As you can see, the public invests a million and makes a profit of $500,000 in six weeks. My agents give their time and services and earn $100,000. The Universal Postal Union collects another $500,000 for their services. The United States post-office sells $2,500,000 worth of stamps and, presumably, makes a profit. The firms or individuals, who buy the stamps from me at a discount, split among themselves a profit of $250,000. France makes a profit of $1,200,000. The holders of French bonds earn another $1,800,000. The enterprises launched with the 15,000,000 francs loaned by the French government, presumably, earn a profit. Not only that but they work for a number of people, who also earn a living. Last but not the least, I make roughly. $65,000 on the deal. If you can show me where the entire transaction results in a loss to anyone, I'll buy each one of you a Stetson hat."

The inspector was flabbergasted. He wasn't prepared to dispute my figures. But he was a hard loser.

"Am I to assume, Mr. Ponzi," he asked, "that you are the unofficial representative in this country of some foreign government?"

"No, Mr. Inspector," I replied with amusement. "Ponzi does not represent anybody but himself. And, furthermore, please bear in mind that we have been discussing only theories and not facts."

The interview at an end, my callers departed much the worse for wear and tear. Personally, I had much to be gratified for. I had won the third round with a hardly a scratch to my debit. I felt liberal and exultant. I turned to my little wife. She was pitifully upset. For her, the interview had been a trying ordeal.

"Never mind, dear," I said to her. "Cheer up and give us a little smile. There is no longer reason for you to be anxious. Lees forget the business and relax. You and I are going to have a nice little supper somewhere, by ourselves, and act like a couple of kids."

CHAPTER XVII

MR. PONZI OPINES THAT, IF GAMBLING IS A SIN, HE'D BETTER HAVE THE CHURCH ON HIS SIDE.

The average man is never satisfied with what he has. He does not realize when he is well off. If he has a shirt, he wants two. If he is single, he wants a wife. If he is married, he wants a harem. (I hope wifey does not read this). He is always reaching for the moon and stepping off into space. Just like I did.

My affairs were then in a fairly good shape. No, I won't say that, either. They were in a bad shape. I was heading toward bankruptcy with the speed of a cannon ball. But I did not know it. Ignorance is bliss.

At any rate, they were not so bad, but that they couldn't be worse. I had plenty of money. And, apparently, the opportunity to clean up a few shekels for myself. But I lacked judgment and caution. I thought I'd reach for more. It was there in plain sight. I did not look beyond it. If I did, I did not see. I must have been blinded by ambition and conceit.

Boston was then coming through gorgeously. Just like a little drum major. The returns were exceeding expectations. That was flattering. But it was dangerous flattery. It made me vain and reckless. It made me dream of wealth, power, popularity, and what not. Oh, what fools we mortals be!

I decided to expand and open branches. In my mind, my venture certainly justified expansion, if any venture did. I was dealing in the most essential commodity of all. I dealt in money. The world was my market. The whole of mankind my clientele.

A contributing factor to my decision to expand, was the obnoxious presence in my office of an old acquaintance. He was in my employ.

Apparently we were friends. Actually, I was in his power. And he was my most dreaded enemy. I feared him. I feared him not for what he could do to me. But for what he might have led me to do to him. Yes. He fully deserved to be "taken for a ride." And I was surely tempted, to buy him the ticket for the journey.

He and I had met before. We had met in a past of which I could never think with either pride or pleasure. We had met in prison. In Canada. In the St. Vincent de Paul penitentiary. Where he was doing a three-year stretch.

When we met again in Boston, several years later, he knew me at once. And remembered. I did too. But he had the drop on me. I was going straight. He was still going crooked. Under the circumstances, I had to capitulate. And, later, give him employment.

The whole thing came about without the least indication of blackmail. He knew better than to make any open, or even veiled threats. His friendly interest in my affairs conveyed to me a clearer message than words. It would have been folly on my part to give him an opportunity to show his hand. That would have precipitated a situation from which I could not possibly have emerged the victor. So, I did the next best thing. I posed as a philanthropist. As a retriever of lost souls. I gave him advice and a job. A pension would have suited me better. But that would have been an acknowledgement of fear.

My employee was a crook by inclination and pursuit. He was one of those prowling, petty, sneaky thieves, whose counterparts in the animal kingdom are the hyenas and the jackals. He would pilfer a poor-box in a church. Pick a drunkard's pocket. Lift anything that wasn't nailed down. Occasionally, with some confederates, he would play a "con" game on some unsophisticated foreigner. The envelope or the handkerchief-switching trick.

At the time I offered him a job, he had just returned from New Jersey, where he had "swindled" a Polish immigrant. The deal had proved somewhat of a financial boomerang. Everything had gone smoothly up to the division of the spoils. These gave him and confederates heart failure. When they opened the envelope supposed to contain their victim's wealth, they found bank notes of fabulous denominations.... But all in German marks, Russian rubles and Austrian crowns! The whole thing wasn't worth 25c a ton! While the envelope they had substituted on their victim contained a few genuine green backs.

He was fit to be tied. In the peaceful atmosphere of my private office, he cursed blue streaks. He cursed the victim, the war, the foreign mints. And everything that was cursable, except himself. He was broke, disgusted and despondent. Perhaps, he was even on the verge of making some rash request. But I anticipated him. I offered him work and a modest salary. Sugar-coating the offer with some fatherly advice as to the errors of his ways. The offer upset his plans, whatever they were. He accepted.

His acceptance may have put an end to his problems. But it only marked the beginning of mine. From then on, I had to find excuses to keep him away from the office as long as possible. A close contact with him was the last thing I wanted. I would rather have hugged a high-tension wire any day.

Between fool's errands and wild goose chases, I managed, somehow, to engage his attentions elsewhere than School Street. Once I even sent him to New York to buy me some choice Hennessey "Three Stars" off the French Line. The "noble" experiment was on. My cellar was dry. And I wanted the stuff badly. But, badly as I wanted it, my fondest wish was that he might get caught with it and "sent up." No such luck! I even bought him a car. Hoping that he might break his neck. He never did. But he did smash the car occasionally. And I footed the bills. That man was as everlasting as sin!

He became my "advance agent" by force of circumstances. I did not want him around. I had to send him somewhere. The further he went and the longer he stayed, the better I liked it. So, I used him to open branches.

People have often commented about the dinginess of my offices. Wondered at the absence of display. At the utter lack of pretentiousness. Some have argued that there was method in my madness. Some have attributed the modest appearances to super-salesmanship. To a keen sense of psychology. But they were all wet. He was my chief reason.

I didn't need branches. I did not want them, I wanted him still less. Since the branches furnished me with a good pretext to keep him out of town, I had to have the branches. But I didn't care to pay for the pretext more than was necessary, hence the dinginess. That is the whole thing "in a couple of nutshells," as between Andy and the King Fish.

Incidentally and accidentally all of my branches turned out to be "gushers." Their very dinginess contributed to their success. Psychologically their modest appearance was a stroke of genius. But I claim no credit for it. I never thought of it in that light. It just happened. Like everything else.

My methods, of course, made State Street see red. Some "buccaneers" of finance are still burning up today at the thought that I stole a march on them. With all of the millions they had invested in the paraphernalia of the "paper hanging" trade, they had to play second fiddle to a "damned little wop" who used ten-penny nails for a coat-rack!

Some of my branches were "knock-outs" right from the start. Others had to be coaxed. From a financial standpoint I didn't care whether I got any returns or not. But from the standpoint of personal pride, I couldn't stand defeat. If a branch was recalcitrant, it was my job to give it a push.

My pain in the neck had dropped in one day to tell me that he had landed one of such lemons. The exact locality does not matter. It was a fairly large community. Within the range of a "Big Bertha" from the Boston Common. Figure that out, if you can!

A branch had been opened there. Everybody in the neighborhood knew it was there. Yet, nobody went near it, and my employee was at his wits' end. So, I drove up there with him to look things over.

I paid a few calls and soon discovered the trouble. Nothing serious. Just a case of "badger game." "Big Business," in the form of a few storekeepers, wanted a "cut in." They had decided that if my proposition was a racket, it should pay for protection. These storekeepers were Genovese. And we have a saying in Italy that it takes seven Gentiles to get the best of a Jew and seven Jews to get the best of a Genovese. The odds were therefore 49 to 1 against me that I would have to come across. I did. I appointed each one of them a sub-agent on a 5% commission. Since they wanted a finger in the pie, I saw to it that they stuck it in up to their knuckles. The deal did not cost me a dime.

My salesman and I finished the day with a social call. I was parched from talking. Dry. "Nobody knows how dry I was!" I was drier than a Methodist conclave.

"Let's go and have a soda," he suggested.

"Nothing doing," I said shaking my head. "I have too much respect for my palate."

"Get yourself a glass of water, somewhere, then," he said.

"Water?" I repeated horrified. "No. I guess not. I see enough of it on Saturday nights. I want some beer."

"Go to Milwaukee," he wisecracked. "It's the nearest place I know of."

"Go to Hades. Do you mean to tell me that you have been in this town a whole month without running across a 'blind pig' yet?" I asked him.

"Well," he stated. "I haven't come across any 'blind ones,' if you want to know."

"What have you been drinking all this time?" I inquired.

"Coffee," he said.

"Oh, yeah?" I sneered. "You look it. What's more I wouldn't believe you under oath. You are holding out on me."

"Holding out nothing," he denied. "The only glass of wine I have tasted here, I got it at the rectory."

"You mean from the priest?" I asked.

"Sure," he admitted. "Who else would be at the rectory? A rabbi?"

"Listen, boy," I told him. "If you know what is good for you, lead me to him. Who is he, anyway?"

"Father ... So-and-so," he replied, mentioning a name, which I immediately associated with my boyhood.

We called at the rectory. We experienced no difficulty in being admitted. In fact, we were received with open arms. The priest and I had never met. But an exchange of data on our respective families disclosed that we were almost related. From then on, we got along first rate. A bottle of the choicest wine made its appearance to help celebrate the event.

In the course of the conversation, it became evident that Father X ... (let's call him that) was interested in my proposition. Even a priest is not above temptation. He wasn't. He pressed me for details and I gave them to him. I described to him the process through which a little dollar could start on a journey across the ocean and return home in six weeks, married and with a couple of kids.

Father X ... was an educated man. What was Greek to others, was just plain English to him. In fact, while I was talking, he was even a step ahead of me. He almost made me gasp for breath with an unexpected remark.

"That would make it exactly $1,350 in three months," he said out of a clear sky.

"Would make what?" I asked, not knowing that he had been doing some mental figuring of his own.

"Thirteen hundred and fifty dollars," he repeated.

As yet, I could not see any connection in his remark. I did not know what he was driving at. I looked at him. He appeared perfectly normal.

"Hold on a minute, Father," I urged him. "You seem to be exceeding all speed limits. Where are you at?"

"I am about a mile ahead of you," be replied with a grin. "I have been figuring that with an initial investment of $600 I could make a profit of $750 in three months."

I nearly swallowed my Adam's apple when I heard that.

"You ... you mean that you want to invest some money with me?" I asked him, still refusing to believe my own ears. A sidekick on the shins from my troublesome employee was not even enough to bring me back to earth.

"Is there any reason why I should not invest with you?" Father X ... asked blandly, while I was still struggling to recover my balance.

"No ... none at all," I assured him promptly. "We have investors in all walks of life."

Further conversation disclosed the fact that Father X did not have any ready cash of his own. But his church had a little nest egg of $600. The fund had been collected for painting and repairs. It was not to be used for three or four months. So, reasoned Father X . . ., why leave it idle, while Ponzi was around to duplicate the miracle of the fishes and the bread?

"You understand that I cannot afford to gamble that money," Father X said to me. "I can only invest it in a safe thing."

"Of course," I agreed with him.

"But that is not all," he continued. "Supposing I needed that money before maturity of the note, what could you do for me?"

"I would return to you the principal upon surrender of the note at any of my offices or through a bank," I assured him. "That is my standing agreement with all of my note-holders."

My assurance proved convincing. Father X... handed over the $600. No one can blame him for that. The temptation was too strong, even for a clergyman. Errare humanum est!

What happened to that money ... I am not telling. Maybe it multiplied I Maybe it dwindled! What difference does it make now? Sooner or later, the church was repaired and painted anyway. If it had to wait, it could wait. Besides, Father X ... and I are still good friends. Amen.

CHAPTER XVIII

MR. PONZI TAKES IT INTO HIS HEAD TO CLEAN UP A FEW BANKS WITHOUT DUTCH CLEANSER

Years ago, and even now, the surest way to get my Nannie was to slight what I call my dignity. I am not stuck up. Never was. I welcome familiarity. Of the right kind. But when somebody tries to put on airs and make me feel like thirty cents, I am off on a rampage.

A rampage does not necessarily mean trouble, I am not troublesome. Not much. Outside of poking a stick in a hornet's nest now and then, I am not really vicious. But I have tongue modeled after the rear-end of a bee. It can sting with vengeance. When I let loose one of my hypodermics, whoever gets it, knows he has been jabbed. "Touché," as they say in France.

Speaking of dignity, that reminds me of the young lady who was catapulted from her saddle over the horse's head. She fell in a heap of disarranged clothes. Jumping to her feet, she was gratified to find herself whole and unobserved.

"Thank goodness! My dignity hasn't suffered!" she said voicing her thoughts with relief.

"I guess it hasn't, maam. Not much," remarked a farmhand who had witnessed the performance from behind a pile of hay, "but you've sure ripped the seat of your pants!'"

My dignity was considerably ruffled one day when a small out-of-town bank insisted that I should furnish references before my account was accepted. That made me hot under the collar. So hot that I actually fumed.

"Gentlemen," I wrote them. "Your request for references is noted and hereby denied. Evidently, our agent has either misunderstood or disregarded our instructions when he offered you our deposit. We deal only with substantial institutions. The size of our accounts is such that we make it a practice never to entrust our money to banks the total resources of which, including building, may be packed into an ordinary club-bag and caused to vanish overnight."

Yours truly, etc."

Eventually, I cooled off and got to think about references. I had a dozen or more of the garden variety. But not one with real background. You know what I mean.

True enough, I had a substantial balance in the Tremont Trust Company. Around half a million. But it was like a ten-carat diamond in a pawn-shop window. It lacked surroundings.

As a reference, the Tremont carried some weight with the common run of people. With the right people. But it enjoyed very little prestige among the blue-bloods. Its president Simon Swig, was Jewish and very much despised by the scions of Mayflower forefathers.

It was a case of State Street versus Salem Street. The two could not mix just like water and oil. And the worst part of it was that Simon Swig was persistently stepping on the Puritan's toes. And making them like it. Because of his strong political connections.

But, in his own way, Simon Swig, was somewhat of a snob himself. He was of the opinion that a Jew was better than a wop any day. I could not agree with him. In my own mind, nothing could be better than a wop. Except two wops. However, we never clashed on racial issues. But, from his attitude, it was evident that he did not care for me beyond the exact figure of my balance. Personally, I didn't give a hoot whether he loved me or not. What I expected from him was service. Not kisses. So, I got none of the latter. And not much of the former, either.

Whenever I gave the name of the Tremont Trust Company as reference to some supercilious investor, I could read a message on his countenance: "Birds of a feather, etc." And I would wince. But I grew tired of wincing. So, I looked around for more flattering connections.

Now, there was, for instance, one of the old aristocratic banks in town. A most exclusive institution. A sort of stepsister to another similar institution, both old timers. Very substantial. But also considerably rapacious. It had a finger in every activity in the State. Controlled both business and politics.

I began to cast longing glances in its direction. But I have always been very impulsive and sudden in my courtings Faint heart never won fair lady. . . . Haven't I married a blue-ribbon? So, one day, I slapped twenty-five one-thousand dollar bills in my pocket. And went to call on the Old Lady to win her favors. She had a reputation of being very distant with strangers. But I discovered that she was a real "coquette" with prospective depositors.

A spotless, speckless and manicured vice-president, with a camel-hair-pencil moustache, noticed me hanging around uncertainly.

"Are you being waited upon?" he drawled with an Oxford accent.

"Not yet," I told him.

"May I assist you, Sir?'" he volunteered.

"I guess so. I only wanted to open an account," I explained.

"I will be delighted to wait upon you, Mr.... er ....I don't believe I got your name," he said.

"My name is Charles Ponzi," I said handing him my card.

He looked at it awhile. Trying to connect the name either with ancient history or modern success. He failed. He set me down as an insignificant.

"What kind of an account do you wish to open, Mr. Ponzi?" he inquired. "Savings or checking?"

"Checking," I replied.

"A business account?" he asked.

"No. just a small personal account," I answered.

The word "small" made him pause and think. I kept on puffing away at my cigarette. He was nervously tapping his desk with a pencil.

"I must be frank with you, Mr. Ponzi," he stated, "but it is the policy of our bank to accept only desirable accounts. We endeavor to give the best of service. We maintain an expensive organization. For that reason, we require checking accounts to show a substantial balance. Are you prepared to meet our requirements?"

"I sincerely hope so," I replied. "By the way, what do you consider a substantial balance?"

"Two or three hundred dollars and up," he said.

"Oh that's reasonable enough," I admitted. "You almost had me scared. You may put me down for an initial deposit of twenty-five."

"Hundreds?" he asked.

"No. Thousands." I replied.

"Twenty-five thousands?" he repeated. "Why ... I thought you said you wanted to open a small personal account?"

"So I did," I acknowledged. "This is about the smallest of my bank accounts."

"Have you any objection to furnish us with the names of your other banks?" he inquired.

I had no objection. I named a few. He took my deposit and left. Apparently, to get me a pass-book. Actually, to check up on me. The moment he came back, I knew he had been doing some telephoning. He was all smiles and attentions. He must have called up the Tremont Trust, among others, and learned of the half a million dollar balance there.

"Here is your pass-book, Mr. Ponzi," he said. "Would you like to have a check book especially printed with your name on it? We will be glad to send you one. If there is anything we can do for you, please command us."

Had there been a whisk-broom handy, that man would have brushed my clothes! And that goes to show that in this world money is yet the best credential of all.

The matter of references satisfactorily disposed of, I began to look around for something to occupy my mind. Just as if taking in money from morning till evening wasn't an occupation. Well, it wasn't. It had gotten to be sort of monotonous to watch my clerks fill the wastebaskets with green-backs, after the cash drawers were full. The money itself meant nothing to me. What I wanted to do was to test its power. To derive from it the thrill incidental to the accomplishment of things called impossible.

I decided to buy banks. It was the logical thing for me to do. I had then accounts in a number of them. All over New England and abroad. And those accounts were surely profitable to others. Earning dividends for others. So, why not make them profitable for myself by owning some bank?

My first choice fell upon the Hanover Trust Company. Not because it was better than the rest. But because I had a score to settle with its president. I figured it was a good chance to catch two birds with one stone.

The control of the Hanover could not be bought without much diplomacy. And the control of it could only be had at a price which I had no intention to pay. The stock was not worth more than its market value of $125 a share. And, perhaps, not even that. So, I had to go at it stealthy-like. First of all, I opened there for sixty thousand dollars. A personal account. And I permitted it to grow from day to day up to $500,000 or more. Without drawing against it. I wanted to create the impression that was what is known as a "dormant" account So that the bank officials might feel reassured that there would be no sudden and substantial withdrawals. And might, therefore, invest my balance. Instead of keeping it liquid.

In the meanwhile, through Charles Pizzi, an employee of the bank, and others, I began to buy up small lots of the Hanover Trust's stock. One hundred and twenty-five shares. By paying a few dollars above the market price. But instead of having that stock transferred to me on the books of the corporation, I merely had it endorsed over to me by the stock-holders of record, whose voting proxies I also held.

My next step was to arrange a meeting with the Italian stockholders of that bank. Stabile, Locatelli, Badaracco, DiPietro and one or two more. I told them that I wanted to buy the control of that bank. And get rid of practically all the officers. Whom they had been backing until then. The Italian stockholders were not in a position to buck me just then. It paid them better to have me on their side than against them. We reached an agreement by which all of our shares were pledged to be voted in block on any issue. As I may decide from time to time. That gave me voting control over 600 or more additional shares.

It was not until then that I called upon the officers with a trump card up my sleeve. I strolled down to the bank one day, shortly before 3 o'clock. And stepped into their private office. They invited me to sit down and asked me whether there was anything they could do for me.

"Yes. I think there is," I said. "I have dropped to buy a block of stock in the Hanover and a directorship."

"I believe we can easily accommodate you," one said. "Would you care to buy as many as one hundred shares?"

"A hundred would hardly interest me at all," I replied. "I would like to buy 2,500 or so."

"But the whole capitalization of the bank calls only for 2,000," interrupted the other one.

"The original capitalization, you mean," I corrected. "Are you not offering for sale 2,000 shares of new stock?"

"We have not offered it for sale, yet," said one, a bit surprised, perhaps that I knew of the projected increase of capital, "but we are ready to do so."

"Well, then why not issue it all to me?" I asked.

"We cannot do that because we would be selling you the control of the bank," replied the other.

"That's just what I want," I admitted.

"We are sorry!" said one, "but we cannot consider anything like that."

"We are willing to make you a director," added the other.

"Of what good is that to me?" I asked. "A minority stockholder in a corporation is like nothing at all."

"Do you expect us to surrender that control we have worked so hard to get?" asked the one.

"Do you expect me to place within your unchecked control what my investors entrust to my care?" I retorted. "My millions mean as much to me as your control means to you. My financial standing entitles me to be trusted by you with the control of the bank."

My arguments were not getting me anywhere. They were adamant in their determination to keep the control. But I was equally determined to take it away from them. I looked at my watch. It was about ten minutes to closing time. It was my chance to play trumps. And I led one.

"It seems to me," I said, "that our differences cannot be bridged. Let's drop the subject. Keep your bank and I'll look for another one."

I pulled out my checkbook and started to make out a check.

"Can you tell me what my balance is today?" I asked and they understood right away what I was after. "You are not going to withdraw your balance, Mr. Ponzi?" The officers asked considerably perturbed.

"Certainly, I am going to withdraw it," I replied. "Right now."

"But it is hardly fair for you to do that," the other remarked. "You have a large balance and should give us notice."

"Why? My money is on a checking account. Is there any reason why I shouldn't write checks to the extent of my balance?" I inquired.

"No. You have a perfect right to do that," they agreed. "But a bank does not usually keep such a large amount of liquid cash on hand. We would have to dispose of some securities, probably, at a loss in order to honor your check."

"That does not concern me," I insisted.

"Why can't we get together and compromise?" it was suggested by one.

"What have you got to offer?" I asked.

"We will sell you 1,000 shares of the new stock," he replied.

"Nothing doing," I told him. "That would be like throwing good money after bad money. We cannot get together on that basis." "But we don't own that many shares ourselves," pleaded one of them.

"Perhaps, not," I conceded, "but you control more than you own."

"We are willing to sell you as many shares as we control," said one. "An equal number. No more. No less. The independent stockholders will vote with whatever side they see fit."

"How many shares do you think you control?" I demanded to know.

"Not over 1,500 all told," he stated. "We will sell you 1,500 shares."

Both were banking on their control of the Italian stockholders who, in the past, had always voted with them. They didn't know that those stockholders were now pledged to me. While I knew that 1,500 shares would have given me a substantial majority.

"Do you also agree to make me a director?" I asked them.

"Yes," it was affirmed. "We will call a special meeting so that you may be elected director and a permanent member of the executive committee."

"I have also a couple of friends I want in the board of directors," I stated.

"All right, we will concede that too."

"Fine!" I said. "I'll take the 1,500 shares."

Half an hour later, I left the Hanover Trust with certificates for 1,500 shares of the stock. The bank was mine! With everything that stood in its name. Including the 12 or 14 story building - the Journal Building, so called,- at the corner of Water and Washington Streets. In which the Hanover Trust Company was located.

With a little over $2,000,000 I had gained control over resources amounting then to about $5,000,000. Not only that, but I had the officers by the small of their neck. Those same officers a few months before, had refused me a $2,000 loan because my account "was more of a bother than a benefit." Oh Boy! Didn't it feel good to know that I could now tell them a thing or two!

CHAPTER XIX

MR. PONZI GOES SHOPPING AND BUYS A MILLION DOLLARS' WORTH OF SUNDAY PARCELS.

To buy a bank is no trivial incident. Even a comparatively small bank. Like the Hanover Trust Company. A man, after he gets to the point where he owns a bank, calls it a day and quits. If he is an average man. Of course, topnotchers don't quit. They never do. But you wouldn't call them the average men. They are out of the ordinary. Professional, in their line. They gobble up banks faster than a turkey does mush. And their gizzards never feel congested.

I don't know anything about the condition of my own gizzard. After I bought the Hanover. It didn't feel congested. Just the opposite, rather. It felt as empty as if it was missing. In fact, I developed an awful appetite. I wanted to buy everything in sight.

I put my hooks out for the Prudential Trust Company. Its president thought he could give it to me for the price of the Custom House Tower. He didn't get to first base. I knew he was heading for a crash. And all I had to do was to stretch out my arms, to catch him before he struck the ground. Nevertheless, I made him a liberal offer. He turned it down. And crashed. Only, I wasn't there to catch him when he did.

In rapid succession, I bid on the Lawrence Trust Company, of Lawrence. On the Carney Building, in Tremont Street. And other properties. I bought myself a house in Lexington. One in Winthrop. A small apartment building in the West End. I took half-dozen mortgages here and there. Purchased a substantial interest in the C. & R. Construction Company. A hundred shares in the old South Trust Company. A few in the Fidelity Trust Company. In the Tremont Trust Company. I even bought myself the Napoli Macaroni Company. So that I wouldn't run out of spaghetti at home.

The more I bought, the more I wanted to buy. It was a mania. A frenzy. I almost bought the Niles Building. The one in which I had my office. It seems that the other tenants had been kicking. They claimed they couldn't get to their offices. Because my investors blocked the entry, the elevator, the stairs and the corridors. O'Brien, the superintendent of the Niles Building, sent for me.

"I am sorry, Mr. Ponzi," he said. "But if you can't regulate the crowd that comes to your office, I have to give you notice to move."

"I am equally as sorry, Mr. O'Brien," I told him. "But I shall not move."

"You can't expect me to lose the other tenants on your account," he protested.

"I should worry about them!" I replied. "Let them move. I'll take the entire floor."

"But your people are blocking also the entry and the stairs," he complained.

"Oh, all right. Let's not argue over it," I said. "Name your price and I'll buy the building."

The superintendent could find no words in reply. He knew I had the money. And was crazy enough to go through with the deal. just to win my point. I don't know how he managed to satisfy the other tenants. But I didn't move.

The day I couldn't buy something, I felt actually disappointed. An auto salesman caught me in that mood one afternoon.

"I have a car," I told him.

"A good car?" he asked me with a bit of sarcasm.

"What do you think?" I retorted. "Do you suppose I drive around in a wheel barrow?"

"I have been told that you own a Hudson," he said.

"It's very true," I admitted. "And I am very much satisfied with it."

"But you need a much larger and more expensive car," the salesman urged.

"What, for instance?" I asked. "What are you selling, anyway?"

"Locomobiles," he replied, spreading an open folder in front of me.

I looked through it. Found the picture of a car that. caught my fancy.

"How much for that?" I inquired pointing out to him the one I wanted.

"$12,600 delivered," he replied:

"All right," I said. "Send it right over. I'll take it."

"But I cannot deliver that car now," he said.

"When can you deliver it?" I wanted to know.

"In about three months," he answered.

"Too late," I told him. "I want that car right away."

"That car isn't even finished," he said. "It's being made to order for a New York millionaire."

"When will it be ready?" I asked. Knowing by then that the car was hard to get, I wanted it. Just to put something over the New York millionaire.

"In about two weeks," he told me. "It must be-delivered by July 1st."

"Fine!" I exclaimed. "Have it downstairs, in front of the door, by July 1st."

"But that car is already sold," he tried to persuade me.

"Listen, young man," I warned him. "I want that car. And when I want something, I am prepared to pay for it. Have that car here by not later than one o'clock, July 1st, and I will give you $1,000 more for it."

That particular car was delivered to me on schedule. At 15 minutes to one o'clock, July 1st, 1920.

Things like that were common. They happened every day. Some involved little money. Some were more expensive. Like the car. Like anything else. Because it gave me a thrill to, pose as a Count of Monte Cristo. To be able to walk in anywhere and tell the man in charge: "Wrap it up, please. I'll take it." Regardless of whether the item was a box of candy or a building.

One day I walked down to the market district. I went in. Where I had been working less than two years before. I wanted to see the boys and the girls. My former co-workers. I stopped to chat with each of them. Then I walked into Poole's private office. He was not expecting my visit. And much less what I had in store for him. Nor did he know that I was a millionaire. He had heard that I was doing pretty well.

"Have a seat, Charlie," he said. "They tell me that you're in business. Dealing in some sort of foreign securities."

"That's right," I admitted.

"How are you making out?" he inquired.

"Fairly good." I replied. "That's what brought me here. To get your advice. I have a few dollars I would like to invest."

"Why don't you buy a few shares of my preferred stock," he suggested. "It pays 7%."

"I would rather have some common," I told him. "It ought to pay more."

"I'll tell you what I'll do," he said. "I will give you 25 shares of each."

"Is that all?" I complained. "It seems hardly enough to bother with it."

Poole looked kind of puzzled. He didn't know whether I was fooling or in earnest.

"How much more stock do you want?" he asked.

"I'll take all you have," I replied indifferently.

Poole laughed. He was amused. Thought it was a pretty good joke. Coming from an ex-employee of his. But he pitied me a little, at the same time. Thinking I was sort of looney.

"Listen, Charlie," he said, trying to break it to me gently. "It takes a lot of money to buy this company."

"I figured it would," I agreed. "That's why I have waited this long to call on you. I was afraid I wouldn't have enough."

"And you may still be short of the mark," he commented skeptically. "However, if you can afford them, you may have 500 shares of preferred for $47,500 and 200 shares of common for $35,200."

"Do I get with it a directorship in your company?" I asked.

"Yes, you can have the directorship too," he agreed, still believing in his own heart that I was only bluffing.

"In that case, have the certificates made out," I told him.

"Where is the money?" he asked.

"Right here," I said pulling out a check-book.

I made out the check. Handed it to him. He took it. And looked sort of sheepish. He knew the check was good.

"I didn't think you meant it," he said.

"J. R., I never bluff," I told him, and taking from my wallet six certified checks made out to me for $200,000 each, I spread them before his eyes.

"Good Lord!" he said. "That's $1,200,000!"

"Yes, and there are several more millions back of them," I assured him.

A few days later, I bought from Poole the remaining 550 shares of common stock. Paying for it about $206,000. And I loaned the company another $155,000. Poole and I had agreed to increase its capitalization to one million dollars and open branches in several foreign countries.

The deal added to the variety of my holdings. It gave me a sardine factory up in Maine. And a meat packing plant out in Kansas City. Both owned by the J. R. Poole Company. I must have felt in my bones that the depression was coming. Because with what I took over I certainly made preparations to cope with it!

Not only was I buying right and left. But I also was opening branches all over creation. I had 35 of them in New England. I had large accounts in about 45 banks. I was going like a house afire!

People must have thought I had discovered the buried treasure of the Incas. Or Aladdin's lamp. If they gave a thought at all to the coupons, they must have got dizzy figuring how many of them I needed to justify what I was doing. In fact, my visible resources were then in excess of $5,000,000. Assuming I earned two cents on each coupon, I should have had to handle over 250,000,000 of them! It was absurd. There were not that many in the world. There had never been that many. And it would have taken months to print them!

The long and short of it is that, for some time, I had not been getting any coupons at all. In fact, after the first lot, I had not been able to buy any more. Except in small quantities. For no other reason than the existing supply was not sufficient to meet the increased demand. They had to be ordered from the Universal Postal Union. But the moment the postal administrations of the various countries concerned began to notice an unusual activity in coupons, the cat was out of the bag. One by one they took step to suspend the sale of coupons.

I learned of it soon. Sooner, in fact, than official Washington. But not soon enough to get out from under. Confident that the coupons were on the way, I had redeemed a number of my notes with cash derived from the issuance of new notes. When the coupons failed to arrive, I found myself in the position where I could not have met all of my outstanding notes in full. Not only I couldn't pay the promised 50% return. But I couldn't even refund the principal at more than 75 cents on the dollar.

"What was I going to do? Proclaim my insolvency and face prosecution, or keep up the bluff and trust to luck. I kept up the bluff, hoping that I might eventually hit upon some workable plan to pay all of my creditors in full. It never occurred to me to pocket all the ready cash and duck out. If I had, I wouldn't have been called the darn fool as many times as I have been.

Fortunately a darned fool had no occasion to he lonesome, any-where. He generally finds plenty of company, just like I did, and in the most unexpected places. That why I managed to survive a few months longer.

In fact, one morning the postal inspectors paid me a call; one of the regular calls, I should say, because they had been in the habit of dropping in every now and then. The moment I saw them I could tell by their countenances that they had something up their sleeves and they had too. But that something might as well have been "arm-bands," for all the good it did them. However, their buoyancy put me on my guard.

"Mr. Ponzi," said one, "we have found that some of your statements cannot be reconciled with certain advices that we have received from the department."

"Which is equivalent to say that since you would not dispute the department, I must be a liar," I remarked.

"No, no," he hastened to assure me, "but we have come to hear what explanations you may have to offer."

"On what subject?" I asked.

"On the subject of your purchases of coupons," he replied. "Where do you buy them?"

"I am not telling that," I replied, refusing to commit myself. "I will merely say that they can be profitably bought in any country having a depreciated paper currency."

"For instance?" he insisted.

"For instance, Italy, France, Rumania, Greece, and so forth," I answered.

"Exactly," he said. "Now we have information that Italy, France and Rumania have withdrawn from the postal agreement and stopped the sale of coupons since March 31st."

"You are not telling me anything new," I retorted. "That information was sent out some time ago by your department to every post office and I have copies of the bulletin."

"Do you admit that coupons cannot longer be purchased in those countries?" he asked, trying to pin me down.

"No, I cannot admit that," I answered. "I may admit, if that helps you that they are no longer for sale to the general public. But I have every reason to believe that my orders are not being turned down anywhere."

"If that is so, it is being done without the knowledge of those governments," he stated.

"Perhaps so," I agreed, "but that is no concern of mine. All that I am interested in is in getting them."

"Assuming that you may still obtain the coupons, how are you going to redeem them?" he inquired.

"The same as usual," I replied. "By presenting them at the post-office."

"But all postmasters have been instructed not to redeem coupons issued by those countries after March 31st," he maintained.

"What of it?" I rebutted. "If the coupons are still obtainable in those countries, regardless of all regulations to the contrary, it would be an easy matter to have them stamped with a date prior to March 31st."

"Do you mean to say that you have connections with some postal officials who are disloyal to their governments?" he kept on, crowding me.

"I don't mean to say anything of the kind," I replied. "I am merely showing you how certain difficulties can be overcome. You may draw all the inferences you want."

Just then Al Ciullo came in the office. A friend. Fate had sent him. He did not know the two men with me were inspectors. He had no idea of what we were talking about.

"Charlie," he said, interrupting the conversation and handing me an envelope with about 300 international reply coupons. "I have just received this package of coupons from Italy."

I took them out of the envelope. Looked them over. And smiled. The two inspectors turned upon him like lightning.

"Where did you get them?" they asked him.

"I got them from my uncle in Italy," Ciullo replied.

"Who is he?" the inspector pressed on.

"He is a postmaster in a small town," Ciullo told him.

"When did you receive them?" the inspector fired at him.

"This morning," he stated.

"How?" the inspector went on.

"By mail," said Ciullo.

"Let's see the envelope," the inspector asked me.

I handed the envelope to him. He examined it carefully. Looked at the cancellation mark. It bore a May date.

"Well," I told the inspector with a bit of sarcasm, "I hope you are satisfied now that somebody else beside myself can buy coupons in Italy. Even if it is two months since March 31st."

"I'll be damned!" said the inspector departing with his running mate. He had seen enough to give him a fit.

Regardless of the difficulties which had developed, I did not abandon all together the idea of buying coupons. I knew human nature. I knew the weak point of public officials. I knew that money talks everywhere. And I proposed to make it talk.

The president of the Hanover Trust Company was a sort of unofficial representative of the Polish government. Whether actually or allegedly, I don't know. But he seemed familiar with events in Poland. And in a position to approach government officials of that country. In the course of a conversation, he mentioned to me that Poland was trying to negotiate a $10,000,000 loan in the United States.

That, gave me an idea.

"Henry," I said to him, "this is your chance of a life-time to clean up some real dough."

"How?" he asked.

"Get in touch with the right parties in Poland," I told him, "and fix it so that they sell me enough international reply coupons for the equivalent, in their own money, of $10,000,000. I can give them the ten millions inside of two weeks. And I am willing to take delivery of the coupons over a period of six months."

"I may put the proposition up to them," he agreed. "But I don't know what success I'll have."

"Listen, Henry," I said to him. "Public officials are very much the same the world over. Go to it. I am no piker."

While he undertook to cover the Warsaw's end of the deal, I took care of the Washington's end. It was as important to redeem the coupons as it was to buy them. But the deal involved such a large number of them that only the Postmaster General himself could handle it.

I instructed my attorney to get in touch with him. He did so. Through Congressman Peter Tague. And in a few days the congressman wired back that the Postmaster General Burleson had pronounced the transaction entirely legal. Not only that, but the congressman, whom I met shortly after in the Parker House, told me that Postmaster General Burleson had also agreed to redeem $1,000,000 worth of those coupons a mouth.

CHAPTER XX

MR. PONZI, HEADING FOR THE ROCKS, MANAGES TO STEER CLEAR OF THEM FOR A WHILE.

The Polish deal fell through, as he could not deliver the goods, and I was left high and dry; with no coupons and no profits in sight, and no way of meeting my notes, except by the time-honored custom of robbing Peter to pay Paul. I was a case of either sink or swim, and I admit that I didn't want to sink. Not just yet, in any event, as I figured that as long as there was life there was hope, and I hoped.

Because of that, I have been called an optimist, a dreamer, a visionary, and everything else, including a crook, probably on account of the fact that I didn't get away with it, like many of the bankers I know of and like some of the big corporations I know of. If I had, they would have called we a genius; a wizard, without the quotations marks.

To hope, meant to fight; to fight for my self-preservation. I was threatened with destruction; not by the government or any group of interests and not by any individual, but by an order of things which I had elected to challenge. Let's not make any bones about it. Nobody was responsible for the fix I was in; nobody but myself, even though I might have walked right into it in good faith.

My exact predicament was that every time I paid one of my notes, through the issuance of another note, I added about 75% to my indebtedness, instead of decreasing it. That means that for each $100 borrowed in December, 1919, when I started out, by compounding 75% every six weeks, I owed in August, 1930, about $2,000. Proportionately less, for every $100 borrowed since, but a huge sum nevertheless.

The predicament was relatively critical. With four or five million dollars in cash and every opportunity to beat it for parts not reached by extradition treaties, it could not be called critical. It was ideal. But for a stubborn cuss like me, determined to stick it out to the end, it was more than critical. It was hopeless.

On the other hand, four centuries before, Columbus had started out from Spain on what he thought was the western route to Asia and the East Indies. On the way over he had discovered America. He didn't know that it was there, and nobody else knew it, except the Indians. Yet, he ran smack right into it.

I felt about the same way. I knew what I was up against if I stopped. I knew not what I might run across if I kept on. I had an unlimited confidence in luck, as well as in my ability to exploit it. And on I went headlong, like a bull in a china shop, to smash all precedents and principles of high finance as it was preached, but not practiced, in Wall Street.

I believed myself able to cope with any eventuality except death, and that was the last thing I should have worried about. Instead, it was the first thing because I wanted to protect my creditors as well as my family. The answer was life insurance. I decided to take out a sort of a blanket policy large enough to cover all of my outstanding liabilities. And increasing it from time to time, so as to keep abreast of them.

Acting on the impulse, as I always do, I phoned immediately to an insurance agent. He was in my office inside of ten minutes.

"I'll tell you what I want," I said to him. "I want a policy on my life for a year for an amount in excess of my outstanding notes. I also want the privilege of increasing that amount from time to time and to renew the policy for another year or more. The policy must be made payable to some bank. Let us say the First National Bank. As trustee for my noteholders."

"What is your purpose?" the agent asked me.

"My purpose," I explained to him, is that, in the event of my death, my creditors be paid in full out of the policy, leaving my entire estate intact to my family. Free from any impediments. For that reason I want the policy for an amount always larger than what I owe. As my liabilities will grow, I must increase accordingly the amount of my policy."

The insurance agent left promising quick action. I went down to the first National Bank. And put the proposition to the vice-president, in charge of the Trust Department. He approved it and we both went to attorney Blodgett's office to have a regular agreement drawn up.

This instrument, after a series of "whereases" which recited how Ponzi, the manager of the Securities Exchange Company, was engaged in a business dealing with international reply coupons, in the furtherance of which he was borrowing money from the public at a rate of interest of 50% every 45 days, appointed the First National Bank of Boston beneficiary in trust of a life insurance policy of the amount of several million dollars, out of which in the event of Ponzi's death, the said bank agreed to redeem all of the outstanding obligations of the Securities Exchange Company, as evidenced by notes similar in tenor and description to the sample attached to the agreement.

Having settled the problem of death, I turned to those dealing with my every day life. I was being constantly investigated. That was a nuisance. I couldn't put a stop to it. The postal inspectors were persistent. They were slowly creeping up on me. With a volume of data hard to beat. But they were up against it too. Even if my claim that I was dealing in coupons was fraudulent, the way I redeemed my notes precluded prosecution. Prosecution could not begin until I defaulted my payments. However, I had to be always on my guard.

The state authorities were not generally nosey. Or troublesome. But now and then they would show signs of life. And cause a little excitement.

One morning, for instance, I received a telephone call from my agent in Manchester, N. H. He told we that the Insurance Commissioner had forbidden him to continue operation until he had obtained a license. The matter was serious. It threatened my entire structure. A defeat in New Hampshire would have invited attack from all of the New England states where I maintained branches. I jumped into a hired car and drove to Manchester.

On my arrival there, my agent gave me the details of the occurrence. Then we went to my banking headquarters and conferred with one of the officers there.

"I am glad you came over," he said to me. "Because the situation is particularly dangerous and must be handled skillfully."

"Is there any inside story to it, beside what Bruno has already told me?" I asked him. Bruno was my agent.

"Yes," he replied." "In fact, it is mostly inside work."

"Politics?" I suggested.

"Some," he admitted. "But pressure from financial interests, more than anything else."

"Do you know the source?" I asked him.

"Not with a mathematical certainty," he answered. "But I can guess. There is, perhaps, more jealousy among banks than among other competing organizations. And it is well known that we are one of your depositors and that you carry a large balance with us."

"But, undoubtedly, you must have a pretty good idea how to handle the situation?" I hazarded.

"I have," he admitted. "Probably as much as anyone else."

"What do you advise me to do?" I asked.

"My advice is that you retain a prominent attorney to handle both the legal and any other aspect of the matter," he suggested." "It may be a little expensive, but it will prove worth while in the end."

"Have you any particular attorney in mind whom you may recommend?" I inquired.

"Yes," he said. "Go and see this attorney in this building, mentioning my name. Bruno will come with you. He knows him."

Bruno and I went upstairs to call on the lawyer.

"We must take the position that your business does not come within the scope of the Blue Sky Laws," he advised, after having listened to me.

"Precisely," I agreed.

"The commissioner contends that Bruno should submit an application for a license," he went on analyzing the case. "But an application requires a detailed account of your business secrets, such as, I am sure, you would not care to divulge. So, an application is out of the question. We will dispute his jurisdiction."

"Can we conclude the matter today?" I asked.

"I hope so," he said. "We will start immediately for Concord and have a conference with the insurance commissioner."

The lawyer was some driver! At the wheel of his Stutz he just ate up the road. Regardless of the curves and anything else I never flirted as close to a crash as I did that day. He would have broken all records down at Daytona Beach!

In Concord, the commissioner gave us an immediate hearing. He and my attorney had some lively controversies. But the conference ended as conferences generally do. The commissioner took the matter under advisement.

The commissioner drove back to Manchester with us. And I had him all to myself on the rear seat during the return trip. We talked. The commissioner was very much interested in the operations of the Securities Exchange Company. He enjoyed the details. And I did not miss the opportunity of painting a pretty picture for his benefit. In Manchester, we parted.

In the evening, Bruno and I called again on my attorney there by appointment.

"Well, what are the latest developments?" I asked him.

"I have had a long talk with the commissioner after you left," my attorney replied, "and he seems inclined to concede that he has no jurisdiction."

"Good for him!" I burst out. "When will he announce his decision?"

"Perhaps, tomorrow," my attorney said. "He was telling me that he was very impressed with the explanation you gave him on the way back from Concord."

"Really?" I said.

"Yes, he confirmed." "In fact, I am personally convinced that he would not hesitate to make a small investment with you."

"That sounds too good to be true," I stated. "Can you arrange that?"

"I doubt it," he replied. "Because he has no money."

"Heck! That does not matter," I told him. "He can have one of our notes without paying a cent for it. The pleasure of having his name on my books is worth more than money to me."

"Do you want him?" my attorney asked.

"Do I want him?" I replied. "Just listen to that! Do I want him? I want him so badly that I simply cannot live without him!"

"I believe I can fix that," my attorney promised. "But it would never do to issue him a note without a proper consideration Let's do the thing right."

"I am listening," I said.

"You and Bruno arrange it so that the Commissioner may borrow some money from the bank," he suggested. "Let him invest what he borrows and when he collects from you he can pay back the bank's loan."

"That's easy," I agreed. "How much shall I let him have?"

"Shall we say two thousands?" said my attorney.

"O.K. with me," I replied. "We will go right down to the bank and arrange it."

The bank readily agreed to loan the commissioner $2,000 on his personal note, with the understanding that Bruno would have guaranteed the loan.

"Well, how did you come out?" one of the bank employees asked, meaning the hearing.

"I think we won the day," I replied to him.

"Is the commissioner going to give Bruno a license?" he inquired.

"I don't think so," I told him. "He seems to agree that he has no jurisdiction. By the way, is the commissioner's credit any good at your bank?"

"I hardly think so," the bank employee answered. "His financial circumstances are rather limited."

"Well, it does not matter," I said. "I want you to let him have $2,000 on his personal note for sixty days. Bruno will stand responsible for the loans. Is that satisfactory?"

"Entirely," he agreed. "I'll let him have ten thousand, if you say so."

"No. Two thousand will be enough" I told him. "When his note comes due, if he does not pay it, just have it charged to Bruno or to my account."

"May I ask the purpose of the loan?" inquired the bank employee.

"Sure," I replied. "He is going to invest the $2,000 with me."

"That is certainly rich!" said the bank employee laughing.

When I left Manchester that evening, I had accomplished more than I had hoped. Two days later, the insurance commissioner announced that my agent did not need a license. Right after that, he went to the bank. The attorney also went to the bank and drew out some money. His own money. Fifteen thousand dollars. And also invested them with Bruno.

Shortly after the Manchester incident, I was "invited" to participate at a conference in the office of the Commissioner of Banks in Massachusetts. I could have declined the "invitation." The commissioner had no way of compelling my attendance. But, on the other hand, I couldn't very well stay away and let him think that I was afraid. After all, his questions were not apt to embarrass me. What he didn't know about coupons and foreign exchange would have filled a good sized library.

I went up to the State House and was ushered right into his office. In those days, I did not have to warm my heels at anybody's door. The Bank Commissioner greeted me cordially. Almost effusively. Like a cannibal greets a missionary. Because he knows he is going to have him "for" dinner, chopped up in little pieces, like Hungarian goulash. I could almost see him smacking his lips in anticipation. The Bank Commissioner, I mean, not the cannibal.

The table was all set. The "guests" were seated. That is, a couple of assistant attorneys general and a foreign exchange expert from one of Boston's banks. Not much of an imposing gathering. The Commissioner himself, I felt, was not conversant with foreign exchange and the two assistant attorneys general didn't know more about the law than the man whose assistants they were. The foreign exchange expert was like the rest of experts. He had the gift of expressing what he didn't know in a way that nobody understood. That's why he made a hit every time he opened his mouth.

After one glance at that conclave, I knew it was a cinch. I was almost ashamed to match wits with them. It was like stealing candy from a baby. But they were the challengers. And I couldn't very well let them get away with their lollypops.

The conference didn't last long. It couldn't. My opponents ran out of arguments even before I was half through with mine. The foreign expert had to admit that my claims as to foreign exchange were correct. The two assistant A. Gs. had acknowledge that my activities were not in violation of any state law. The Bank Commissioner had to concede that my company did not come within his jurisdiction.

We parted the best of friends. Sorry, in fact, that we couldn't chum around oftener.

One of the assistant attorneys general was actually hooked. He drew me aside and told me that he wanted to come down to my office and invest some money. The Bank Commissioner was non-committal on that subject.

"Why don't you come up and see me sometime?" I think he said, or words to that effect. But, in any case, he left out the "dark and handsome." Afraid, perhaps, that Mae West might call him a copy cat.

CHAPTER XXI

LADIES STOP "RUNS" WITH LUX, BUT MR. PONZI STOPS ONE WITH A MILLION DOLLARS

Things were happening fast and thick in my office. I didn't have a minute to myself from 9 a.m. till 5 p.m. And life was one surprise after another. Some pleasant, some unpleasant, but most of them amusing, because I had a sense of humor and still have. I have lost everything, but that.

One morning, as I was going through my mail, a caller was announced - a member of the Massachusetts Senate. I had him come in.

"I am the spokesman for a group of friends," he opened up. "We have gotten together and subscribed a large sum for the purpose of buying one - half interest in your business."

"But I have no intention to sell even an eighth of an interest," I informed him.

"We anticipated that," he stated, "and for that reason I am authorized to offer you one million dollars. We are ready to deposit the amount, in evidence of our good faith and agree that it he paid over to you after you have disclosed to us the secrets of your enterprise."

"My dear senator," I told him, "your figures do not stagger me at all. Your little million pales into insignificance before my weekly receipts of twice that amount. Besides, what could prevent you from learning my secrets and using them to your own advantage without paying for it?"

"Our own honor and respectability," he replied. "We are all men of the highest character."

"I don't dispute that at all," I assured him. "On the other hand, experience has taught me not to gamble on people's character. I am sorry, senator, but your little million cannot buy anything around here. It is not even attractive as a loan. Good day, senator."

As he went out, a police inspector from headquarters came in. He said he had received a complaint from a Mrs. Campbell. "What's the nature of her complaint?" I asked him.

"She claims," he replied, "that you induced her to invest some money with you and her friends told her she would lose it. She wants her money back."

"Legally, she cannot force me to redeem my note before maturity I told the inspector." "And there is nothing you can do about it. But since it has always been my policy to refund money to dissatisfied investors, tell her to come down and get hers."

"Will you give it to her?" he inquired.

"Of course, I will," I assured him, and he left.

He came back with Mrs. Campbell a little later. He handed me the note and I instructed my secretary to give her a check. When she saw that she was going to get her money, Mrs. Campbell changed her mind.

"Mr. Ponzi," she said, "I am awfully sorry I did you an injustice, but my friends led me to it. I want to leave the money with you until maturity."

"What?" interrupted the inspector. "After making all that fuss and putting me to all that trouble, you don't want your money now? You may do as you like, but I am through handling your case." He started to leave, but I asked him to stay.

"Please remain until this thing is closed," I urged him. Then turning to Mrs. Campbell, I said:

"I am sorry, but now you must take your money. I do not want it. I do not care to have as investors persons who have no confidence in me. Go back to your friends, show them your money and thank them for the services they have rendered you. Good day, madam."

"Mr. Ponzi," said the inspector shaking hands with me, "I am sorry for any inconvenience my call might have caused you. I have witnessed how you do business, and from now on, if any person comes to me with a complaint against you I'll show them that I know how to handle it."

"I am glad that you came," I told him. "It was no trouble at all. What you saw me doing for Mrs. Campbell, I am always ready to do for all my investors." But I was hoping and praying that I might not be called upon to do it, because I couldn't have gone all the way around.

However, if Mrs. Campbell was nervy, the Chief of Police of a small Massachusetts town was not shy either. He had more gall than a brass monkey. He came to my office one day and said that he wanted to invest. He told me that he had no money.

"Well, what do you want to invest then?" I asked him. "Your badge?"

"No," he said, "I thought I would give you my note for $500. You could discount it at your bank."

"Fine business," I exclaimed. "And you expect me to use my bank credit for you whether you have the money or not, and pay you 50% for it besides?"

"Well, it wouldn't cost you anything," he argued back, "and it is the same for you whether you get your money from me or from the bank."

"Listen, Chief," I told him, "I won't argue with you because I can put my time to better advantage, but it strikes me funny that you should come here and take me for a sucker so I am inclined to do just what you ask. Here, sign this note for $500 and I will give you ours."

A few days later, some woman reporter, a regular bell cat, stormed my private office and started raving about some friend of hers that I had swindled. "What are you talking about anyway," I asked him, or, pardon me, her. "You know well enough," she replied. "You took $500 away from the Chief of Police all right, and I came here to tell you that if you don't make immediate restitution, I will expose you." "Who is this Chief of Police," I inquired. "I don't seem to recollect the name." "He is the Chief of Police," mentioning the name of a small Massachusetts town, she said, and I couldn't help laughing. "So you claim that I have swindled him, do you?" I asked her. "Yes." she admitted, "I know that you took his money." "Well, let me tell you something, since you are so smart," I told her. "Your friend borrowed from the hand that fed him, from me, the money that he invested."

"I don't believe it," she said.

"I don't give a darn whether you do or not," I assured her, working up a temper. "But here is his note. As to you, since you are so mightily fresh, get out of this office. And stay out."

"Remember, you are speaking to a lady," she warned.

"A person who behaves like you do, is no lady," I told her. Get out or

I'll have you put out. Then, go ahead and expose me as you please."

My day's work was a succession of such incidents. The complaints were few and far between. Practically unknown, in fact. And never justified. But whether justified or not, an investor was never permitted to leave with a grievance for the sake of a few hundred dollars. That's why I lasted as long as I did. If a single complaint had gotten into the courts, it might have wrecked the whole structure.

One day, for instance, a bank messenger came in with five notes of the Securities Exchange Company for $150 each. He presented them for payment to one of the clerks. The clerk brought them to me. I looked at the notes. They were forgeries. I knew how they had gone out of my office. And who had put them in circulation. I could have refused to pay them. But I didn't. I gave the bank messenger $750 and took the notes. It was better for me to lose the money than to lead a bank to believe I was defaulting my payments. Or let the bank know the reason why. There would have been an arrest made. A conviction obtained. But I might have had to take the witness stand and submit to cross-examination. And I certainly wanted everything but that.

Besides investors, all sorts of people wanted to see me. Donation solicitors, for instance. They were thicker than mosquitoes down in New Jersey. And I was fairly liberal with them. Provided they represented some worthy cause. I never hesitated to contribute to labor or soldiers' organizations. But I never gave a dime to build homes for disabled cats. Nor to any stiff-necked reformer. Nor to the anti-saloon league. Although I would have gladly paid some of these "reformers" one-way fare to China, if I could have found a way to keep them there.

Among the donation solicitors, I had one from Ohio. He had come all the way from Marion. But on a wild goose chase. He had picked out a bad day. When I was extremely busy. And it was his hard luck if he wasn't able to see me. Maybe, mine too. Because in those days $50,000 would have gone a long way with the Ohio gang of political buccaneers.

At any rate, what's the use of crying over spilled milk? A clerk came into my private office and handed me a card. I glanced at it. Somebody, whose name I don't remember, from Marion, Ohio.

"Who is he and what does he want?" I asked the clerk.

"I don't know him," the clerk replied. "He said he came from Marion, Ohio, to see you on an important matter."

"Tell him I am sorry," I directed the clerk, "but I am too busy to see anybody."

The clerk departed to deliver the message, but he returned almost immediately.

"Well? What is it now?" I asked him.

"The gentleman says it is very important that he should see you," the clerk informed me.

"I don't give a darn how important it is," I exploded. "I am not going to see him." "Miss Meli," I said turning to my secretary, "you go and see him and tell him to state his business to you. That's the best I can do for him."

Miss Meli, after a short conversation with that man, came back to the office greatly impressed.

"He insists on seeing you personally," she said.

"There can be no such thing as insisting with me," I said. "When I say I won't see him, that settles it. Now, I wouldn't see him even if he was the Czar of Russia."

"But he told me that he was the special messenger of Senator Harding," urged Miss Meli, "and that he was sent by him on a confidential mission."

"Is that so?" I retorted. "Well, tell him I should worry about Senator Harding. I won't see him. I can't be bothered even by a Senator. There are ninety six of them and I cannot create a bad precedent."

Perhaps, I was a little too fresh that day. But who would have thought then that Senator Harding would have become President of the United States? It would have been like betting on a long shot at Rockingham or Narragansett. Still, it would have been a good bet. I might, with a little diplomacy have got in right with the new administration. And, perhaps earned the privilege of bidding against Sinclair for the lease of the Tea Pot Oil Dome.

If I was fresh that day, I had cause to be. I had been told that something was brewing over at the courthouse. And not malt either. Nor hops. But that sort of brew that spells trouble. I was on pins and needles. I wanted to know what it was. To know it ahead. When the Ohio man came, I was waiting for a newspaperman who knew the ins and outs in Pemberton Square.

As soon as he came, we went over together to the courthouse. We made contracts. Obtained the information. And an hour's reprieve. For which I paid with a thousand dollar bill. A real bargain! Because, without that reprieve, the Securities Exchange Company would have met with a premature death.

The whole thing was a million dollar suit brought by an ex furniture dealer. He was claiming to have bought one half interest in the Securities Exchange Company through the $200 loan he had made to me several months before. The suit was not worrying me. But the writ of attachment that went with it, did. Because it covered enough bank deposits to cripple me. In fact, it took in almost $4,000,000 in the Cosmopolitan Trust Company, $700,000 or more in the Tremont Trust Company, $49,000 in the Merchants National Bank of Boston, $10,000 in the First State Bank and about $2,000,000 in the Hanover Trust Company.

The reprieve enabled me to call at most of the banks and juggle things so that only a small part of the funds remained subject to the attachment. I did not bother with the two smaller deposits. But I salvaged three fourths of my account in the Tremont Trust and 90% of the one in the Hanover Trust. At the Cosmopolitan I was told that I was too late. I didn't stop to argue over it. I had to get back to my office before the news of the attachment came out in the papers and prepare myself to cope with the "run" which was sure to follow.

With $3,000.000 in cash in Boston and $3,000,000 more outside of Boston, I faced the music. It lasted a couple of days. In those two days, I refunded about a million dollars. And saved thereby $500,000 in interest, which I would have had to pay at the maturity of those notes. Forty-eight hours were enough to restore confidence. And the million dollars came back again. In less time than it had taken to pay it out.

CHAPTER XXII

MR. PONZI, PEEVED AT THE "MONEY LENDERS," DECLARES WAR ON THEM AND BEGINS HOSTILITIES.

The "run" had resulted in a certain amount of publicity. But that hadn't hurt me a bit. With the general public. Just the opposite. It had served to swell my daily receipts.

In financial circles, however, the publicity had stirred up some jealousy. You know how it is. Bankers hate competition. They fear it. Especially the kind of competition I was responsible for. The best they could offer to their depositors was about 4% a year. While I was not only offering, but actually paying, my investors 50% in 45 days. Or, 400% a year.

Withdrawals of deposits from banks grew in proportion with my cash receipts. The more I took in, the more the banks had to pay out. And the money, once in my possession, would be redeposited only in banks in which I already had an account. Particularly, in the Hanover Trust Company. Because it was my intention to drain several of the banks of liquid cash so as to compel them, eventually, to sell out to me at my own price. All is fair in love and war.

I had it all figured out. The banks could not continue to pay money out and survive. Some might have lasted longer than others. But, sooner or later, all would reach the point where they had either to sell out or close.

A closed bank is generally a total loss to the stockholders. Not only don't they get back what they originally have paid for the stock, but, usually they are also assessed for an additional amount equal to the par value of the stock they hold. In other words, a man who has paid $125 for a share of bank stock, loses not only the $125, if the bank goes in liquidation, but he is often required also to cough up another $125.

I reasoned that, in a pinch of that sort, any bank stockholder would have been tickled to death to sell out to me for about fifty bucks a share. He would have been a fool, if he hadn't. And I was prepared to do just that. Because for every $50 so invested I would have made a profit of $75. Or, in less time than it takes to say Jack Robinson.

How? Why? That's easy! People had confidence in me at that time. They would have rather deposited their money in banks owned by me than in banks owned by somebody else. But, even without new deposits, I could have straightened a bank out by redepositing there, to my name, the money which had been withdrawn by those of its depositors who had invested with me. Since I was not dealing in coupons any longer, since I was not dealing in anything, since money was coming in faster and in larger amounts than I was paying it out, I was in a position to keep my funds idle. Anywhere. And for any length of time. Even if they earned me only 4% a year.

My profit would have come from a different source. From the increased value of the bank stock, after I had bought it at a knocked down price. There was absolutely nothing to it. It was a cinch. I could have bought a bank today at $50 a share and sold a 49% interest in it; a week later, at $125, or better, per share. The public would have gladly bought shares in anything I might own. Not because they were worth more. But because of my name. Of my credit. The same as they were buying my notes.

That would have been one way out of my difficulties. An opportunity to switch, gradually, from the coupons venture into a more conservative line of business. To reduce, a little at a time, the 400% rate of interest I was paying; to get out from under all together, in a non-distant future, and retire a multimillionaire. But I didn't make it. For a number of reasons which I have never bothered since to analyze fully.

Anyway, the publicity I got from the "run" came to the notice of one of my large depositors. It would. I couldn't help it. For a couple of months they hadn't heard anything else but my name. Over the phone. Over the counter. They had seen it in the mail. In telegrams as if it was actually haunting them.

The fact was that, whenever anybody asked me for references, which was often, I gave the name of the bank. Sometimes, I even went into detail. And told how I had a substantial deposit in that bank. Not only, but also how the bank had accepted to be the beneficiary in trust in the matter of my life insurance policy.

From president to messenger boy, everyone in the bank was tired of answering questions about Ponzi. Especially, because they couldn't very well say what was in their mind. And so, one day they sent for me.

I went. I was ushered into some private office. Whose office, I don't know, Whoever the man in that office, was, he came right to the point.

"Mr. Ponzi," he said, "we are besieged by requests for references as to your standing. I am sorry, but we are unable to give any. We don't know a thing about your business."

"Of course, you don't," I told him. "And I don't expect you to tell them what you don't know. But you can tell them that I carry a substantial account here."

"The trouble is that they seem to derive the impression that this bank is in some way associated with your activities," he complained.

"There is nothing I can do to correct that impression," I explained. "What people may think or believe is beyond my control."

"Certainly," he conceded. "But we are placed, nevertheless, in an embarrassing position. For our own protection, I would suggest that you close your account with us."

"It's all right with me," I replied. "Let me have my balance and that will be the end."

"Thank you, Mr. Ponzi," he said. "I shall write you a check right away."

"A check?" I inquired. "Why a check? Let me have the cash, if you don't mind."

"You certainly do not mean to imply that our check is not acceptable to you?" he asked with considerable astonishment.

"I will not go into details," I replied non-committally. "But if you want me to close my account, you will kindly hand over my balance in one-thousand-dollar bills. Forty-five of them, I believe."

He didn't like my attitude at all. But he couldn't refuse me, either. So, he gave me the cash, and I left. Account or no account. I could still use the bank as a reference, because it was the beneficiary under the insurance policy, although that reference was no longer necessary. By then, I had subscribed to Dun and Bradstreet's. And I was rated by them $8,000,000!

The law suit which had resulted in the "run" was taking its course. I had retained Arthur D. Hill to represent me. And I was sure to win out. But, in the meanwhile, I had about three quarters of a million tied up by the attachment. Which, by the way, was not drawing any interest.

That's what set me thinking. Those banks in which my money was tied up, had the use of the funds, without paying for it. The longer the suit lasted, the better it was for them. They were actually the gainers, regardless of how the suit ended.

One of these banks was a small institution in the North End, hardly justifying the name of bank.

I had $10,000 in that bank. I had put them there to help it. The President had begged me on his knees, and as I thought he was a deserving fellow, I had given him the account, which I would have left there indefinitely. But it was subject to my check. And it would have practically ruined the bank if I had asked for my balance, suddenly, and without notice. The attachment afforded him an ideal protection.

As to a larger Trust Company, I had $190,000 tied up there. But they had permitted me to withhold about half million from the attachment, and it was one of the gainers from the suit, yet, to a smaller extent than it could have been.

In another Trust Company, I had $375,000 tied up. The president, refused to release any part of it. And I knew he needed money. Only a short time before he had come to my office and begged me to open an account with his company.

"Mr. Ponzi," he had told me. "You are ruining me."

"How's that?" I had asked him.

"All of my depositors are closing their accounts to invest with you," he explained.

"I am sorry," I had assured him. "I did not think it was as bad as that!"

"It is," he insisted. "For the past week, we have cleared checks to your credit for about $100,000 a day."

"What do you want me to do ?" I had asked him.

"Give me a deposit," he had pleaded.

"But I have my own bank," I had argued.

"I know," he had rebutted, "but do you want to ruin all of the others just for that?"

"No," I had assured him. "I don't want to ruin anybody. I will give you a deposit. I will re-deposit in your bank all of the checks drawn against your bank by any of my investors."

I had done that. But the president was no man of principles. But, of course, I didn't know the kind of a man he was, when I gave him my deposit.

I put him down with others as another who justified suspicion. And I wasn't far from wrong when I did. The attorney for the man suing me was a friend of the president of that bank.

As I was gradually piecing together my clues and bits of evidence, a police inspector from headquarters paid me a visit.

"The president of one of the trust companies was up at headquarters yesterday," he informed me.

"Yes? What was he up to?" I inquired.

"He was raising the devil about you," he said.

"About me?" I asked.

"Yes," he confirmed.

"I thought he was my friend," I remarked.

"Well, he isn't," the inspector assured me. "He says that you are ruining him."

"Of all the nerve!" I exclaimed. "I have about $400,000 tied up indefinitely in his bank and drawing no interest. What more does he want?"

"He wants to have you arrested," he told me.

"Is that so?" I was painfully surprised.

"Yes," the inspector went on. "He raved at headquarters and said that we ought to arrest you."

"And what did you tell him?" I asked.

"We told him that we could not arrest you because we had nothing to arrest you for," he replied.

"And what did he say?" I kept on quizzing the inspector.

"He said that you should be arrested," he answered.

"Is that straight?" I wanted to make sure.

"You know me, Charlie," the inspector remarked.

"All right," I said." "I'll fix that skunk."

"For God's sake, keep me out of this," he begged.

"Don't worry," I assured him. "You have nothing to fear from me."

"I trust you all right," he said. "The boys at headquarters and myself would go to hell for you because we know you are on the level and a regular guy."

What the inspector told me was all I needed to jump right into action. I sent for the man suing me, much as I hated to do it. I dickered with him. I paid him $50,000 in cash to drop the suit. He signed a release. With that, I went right down to the president of the trust company.

"I have come to withdraw my balance," I told him, showing him the release.

"It's too late now," he said. "It's after banking hours. Come back in the morning and I'll have my lawyer examine the release."

"I will do nothing of the kind," I shot back at him. "1 have come here to get my money and I am going to get. it. The man suing me is here. My attorney is here. And the papers are O.K. I will not leave until I have my money. There are 2,000 people outside who want to see how well you can honor your obligations."

"It's after banking hours," he insisted.

"I don't give a darn if it were bed time," I shouted. "You will either give me my money or you will never open in the morning."

"All right," he agreed, "I will give you a check."

"You will give none of your checks," I threw back at him. "Your signature couldn't find credit for a plugged nickel with me. I want cash. All in ten-thousand-dollar bills. Thirty seven of them and a five."

I had to wait perhaps two hours before I finally got my money. And, in the meanwhile, I exchanged a few more pleasantries with both him and the attorney for my suing friend, who had also joined the party. But I walked out of the bank with the money. And in the morning I went right over to the Tremont Trust to get the other $190,000. There, my visit was anticipated. I wonder why? At any rate, I found 19 ten-thousand-dollar bills awaiting me. I stuck them in my pocket, together with the other 37. And I went back to my office. What a nice picking I would have made for some of the stick-up boys of later days! Can you imagine it? A man going around dear old Boston with 56 ten-thousand-dollar bills in his pants-pocket! With six certified checks of $200,000 each in his wallet! With enough smaller bills and gold pieces to buy himself an apartment house! And with only a 25 Colt automatic in his vest pocket!

Even after withdrawing my funds from these banks, I was still as mad as a wet hen. And I wasn't given a chance to cool down. Instead. another bank jumped into the fray. This time, one of the national banks. And my temper went to fever heat.

"'What's the matter now?" I asked them.

"Our drawing bank has notified us that it will decline to do our clearings unless we induce you to place part of your balance on a certificate of deposit."

"What's the idea?" I wanted to know.

"They do the clearings for us," one explained. "You might draw a check on us for several millions and they would have to clear it. This, they claim, they cannot do."

"Ha, ha! I see!" I remarked sarcastically. "So, the highbrows haven't got cash enough to clear my checks? Wouldn't I love, though, to have them turn down one of my checks! Wouldn't I hang their hide up a tree to dry! I am glad of it. Tell them to go to the devil and we will give the story out to the newspapers."

"No, no. We can't do that," said he.

"And why not?" I asked. "Can't we do our own clearings?"

"Not yet," he replied. "We would have to join . . ."

"Well, join whatever it is you have to join," I told him.

"But in the meanwhile we would be left without clearings," he pointed out. "Please don't force us into that situation."

"But you are asking me to tie up my balance," I rebutted. "And I cannot do that because I may need my money at any time."

"You don't have to tie up the whole balance," he said. "Only a part will do. Let's say one million and a half."

I resisted their pressure for a while, But finally I gave in. It seems I couldn't do anything else just then. I walked out of the bank with a certificate of deposit for a million and a half. But madder than ever. And determined to take it out on the whole banking crowd.

The moment I got back to my office, I called up the Bank Commissioner. Made an appointment with him. And went up to the State House.

"Mr. Allen," I said to him, "I have a plan to boost deposits in the Hanover Trust Company, but I desire your approval before I go ahead with it."

"What is your plan?" he asked.

"My plan is to run a sort of contest," I explained to him.

"I am going to offer a prize of $1,000 each month to the person who will be instrumental in bringing to the Hanover Trust Company the largest number of new deposits."

"How are you going to work it out?" he inquired.

"I'll have thousands of cards printed," I told him. Some sort of introduction cards. The contestants will give them out to their friends. Each card will bear the name of the new depositor and the signature of the contestant. It will be turned in with the initial deposit and the bank will pass it along to me or file it. At the end of each month, the cards will be sorted and counted. The contestant with the largest number of cards to his credit will get the $1,000."

"I don't see anything irregular with the plan," admitted the Bank Commissioner. "As a private citizen, you can give out your money as you see fit. But you cannot use the Hanover's funds for it. Or promote the contest in the bank's name."

"I will abide by your directions," I assured him, and left.

I sent for a printer and told him what I wanted. Ten or twenty thousand cards to begin with. And right away. Then I stuck up a couple of notices in my office with the rules of the contest. The war between myself and the banks was on. I had thrown the gauntlet. And I was going right into action to deliver the first blow.

CHAPTER XXIII

MR. PONZI OFFERS UNCLE SAM $200,000,000 FOR HIS SHIPPING BOARD FLEET.

I had not seen the postal inspectors for some time. I had not heard from them. And was wondering whether they had met with an accident. As I had often hoped for. Or, given up the investigation as a bad job. But no such luck. They had been digging up dirt.

In fact, one day the phone rang. The clerk in the outer office answered on the extension. Then he came to tell me that the United States Attorney was on the wire. I lifted the receiver on my desk and announced myself.

"Mr. Ponzi," I heard a voice saying, "this is an assistant United States District Attorney, speaking."

"How do you do?" I greeted him. "What can I do for you?"

"I would like to confer with you," he replied. "Would it be convenient for you to see me?"

"Certainly," I told him. "Where shall I meet you?"

"Could you meet me at my office in Boston?" he asked.

"Yes sir," I answered.

"When?" he inquired.

"Right now, if you want to," I stated.

"I don't want to inconvenience you, Mr. Ponzi," he apologized.

"You are not inconveniencing me at all," I assured him. "I am always glad to place myself entirely at the disposal of the United States Attorney."

That wasn't so at all. I would just as soon see the devil any day.

But a man has to be polite now and then.

That's very nice of you," he commented. The assistant district attorney - I mean, not the devil. "You say you could come now?"

"Yes, sir. I can be at your office inside of ten minutes," I promised.

"Then I shall expect you," he said. "Thank you."

"Don't mention it. I'll be there," I told him.

I went at once to his office. Announced myself. I was ushered into his private office. There, I found one of his assistants, a stenographer, and my two "friends", the post-office inspectors. We exchanged the usual greetings.

"Where is your attorney?" the assistant district attorney asked.

"I have no attorney," I replied.

"Do you mean to tell me that you have come alone to this conference?" he asked.

"Am I threatened with any danger?" I asked back.

"No," he admitted. "But I assumed that you wished to protect your rights. As you know, under the constitution, you are not compelled to speak unless you want to."

"But I have no intention of invoking my constitutional prerogatives," I assured him. "I assume that you want to learn from me something about my activities. I will be only too glad to answer your questions because I have nothing to conceal."

"Mr. Ponzi," he stated, "I am very favorably impressed by your attitude. Do you object to the presence of the post-office inspectors?"

"That's all according to how they behave," I replied with a tinge of humor. "In my office they have forced me to remind them that they were on my premises without authority. However, if they promise to behave, they may remain."

"They are here only in the capacity of spectators anyway," he assured me. "I will conduct the conference."

"All right, then, I agree. Let us get down to business."

The conference lasted about two hours. I reiterated the statements previously made about coupons. I covered the same ground covered at previous conferences. And when the conference was con cluded he seemed pleased. He did not give any indication that he suspected irregularity. If he did suspect, he was keen enough to realize that I had gone into the thing without a criminal intent and was trying my darndest to do the right thing. Even if in a most deplorable way.

The conference with the United States District Attorney did not alarm me. No more than previous conferences with other officials. In fact, why should it have alarmed me? For, nine months I had been under investigation. I had been asked all sorts of questions. And I had been able to answer them all. No action had ever been taken against me. I felt reasonably sure that none would be taken, so long as I kept on paying my notes. At any rate it was too late for me to stop any action that might be contemplated.

I dismissed the conference from my mind. And went along as usual. Meeting events and unexpected situations as they occurred.

One day, I received a hurried call from one of the trust companies. The officer wouldn't tell we over the phone what the matter was. So, I went down to the bank.

"What is the scandal now?" was the first thing I asked.

"We have found a good man for one of your offices," the officer told me.

"For the love of Mike!" I said a bit resentfully. "Is this the important message you had for me?"

"Yes," he admitted with the least vestige of shame. "He is well recommended and will be very useful to you."

"Why didn't you send him up to the office and talk to Miss Meli?" I wanted to know.

"He has been up to your office," he replied. "And you have met him. But it seems that you did not give him much hope."

"Who is he, anyway?" I inquired.

"A young man by the name of, let's say "Smith," he said.

"I'll be darned if I remember him," I remarked.

"Don't you remember a young feller asking you for the Holyoke office?" he asked.

"Oh, yes," I admitted. "I think I do. But I told him that the Holyoke office was already covered."

"Well he is the man," he confirmed, "and you must give him that office."

"What's that?" I said pricking my ears at the word "must."

"I said you must give him that office," he repeated.

"What's the big idea?" I demanded to know. "Why all the pressure?"

"You take our advice and give him the Holyoke office," another officer urged.

"The thing is getting interesting," I had to admit. "What are you so much in earnest for? I have my own man there and I am entirely satisfied with him."

"Well, fire him," one suggested.

"I will, like heck!" I shot back at him.

"Give him another agency," the other suggested.

"Look here," I said. "What is the young man to you, anyway?"

"Nothing," he confessed. "Except that I have been told to get him that office."

"Explain to your friend the circumstances," I told him.

"Impossible," he stated. "I must do as he says."

"That's no reason why I should do as he says," I argued.

"Oh, yes, there is," he answered back.

"Say, are you trying to be funny?" I asked. "There is no man alive who can tell me what to do and what not to do."

"Listen, Charlie," he coaxed. "It's no use to beat around the bush. The 'boss' wants you to give that man the Holyoke office."

"The 'boss'? And who in heck is the 'boss'?" I wanted to know.

"Don't you know?" he asked in surprise.

"No, I don't know," I had to admit.

"Well, for God's sake! Where have you been all this time?" He mentioned one of the men running the state and he was positively amazed at my political ignorance.

"What?" I asked, afraid to have been misunderstood.

"It's just him," he confirmed. "One of the big boys up on the hill."

"Well! ... Well! ... Well! . . ." I said by way of comment. "So, he wants the job covered by one of his friends?"

"I don't like the idea of being bossed," I told him. "But since the big boy thinks enough of my business to become associated with it through his political friends, I believe I will grant the request."

"That's fine!, said he. "So, it is settled?"

"Yes," I assured him. "You can tell the boss that his order will be obeyed right away. And you can also tell that young man to come to my office and arrange the details with Miss Meli. I will wire my man in Holyoke that I have another place for him."

The confidence of the "boss" in my business was rather flattering. I assumed that he would not have urged one of his friends upon me unless he was satisfied, from investigation; that, in his opinion, I was conducting a legitimate enterprise. So, I began to feel hopeful that all government activities against me would soon cease.

Shortly after that, my attention was attracted by an advertisement. Or, some sort of an announcement. The United States government was offering for sale the Shipping Board fleet. An imposing array of some 3,000 vessels which had been built during the war at the tremendous cost of nearly $3,000,000,000! The government was asking $20 per dead-weight ton. They were easily worth $200. Their combined tonnage was approximately 10,000,000. The deal would have involved a lump sum of about $200,000,000!

I took a day off. I went over my data on foreign trade and shipping. Did a lot of figuring. And became convinced that I ought to buy that fleet! I lost no time. Once my mind was made up, I acted. I sent one of my men to Washington with my bid of $200,000,000 and a check for $2,000,000 as a guaranty of my good faith.

In the meanwhile, I began to plan what to do about the money. And with the fleet. In the event it was awarded to me, as it might have been.

In my bid I had mentioned that I would pay cash C.O.D. within 30 days from the acceptance of my bid. An unnecessary haste. Because the government would have been willing to wait ten years for the money. In fact, it waited longer than that. And got nothing for it in the end, from others.

To raise 200 million in 30 days, was not much of a problem, for me. My daily receipts had already reached the million dollar mark. And I was operating only in New England. Or, "on" New England. As some wise guy may say. With requests for agencies from every state in the Union, in 48 hours I could have covered the country from coast to coast, like a radio hook-up.

But that wasn't all. I was getting cables from Indian maharajahs asking we how many millions of rupees I would accept for investment. Cables from Chinese mandarins offering millions of taels. Cables from Australian and South African "gold diggers" tendering millions of pounds sterling. Cables from South America talking about millions of pesos, or milreis, or bolivianos, or sucres, or sols. A lone telegram from a Canadian bank informed me that a Mr. Leyture had deposited with them $7,000,000 to my credit! To raise $200,000,000 under those circumstances would have been a cinch.

I was considerably more puzzled about the fleet. What was I going to do with it? With 3,000 vessels of all sizes? With the Leviathan? With all of the floating Presidents? With the legion of freighters and tankers and tramp steamers? There wasn't much I could do with them. Except re-sell them. So, I lay awake nights studying some selling arguments, some use for the boats, some ways and means to promote a number of subsidiary companies which would take them off my hands.

The fleet was actually going to stand me 320 million dollars. Because, to buy it, I was borrowing 200 million at 50%, through the Securities Exchange Company. And paying agents' commissions amounting to 20 million dollars. I devised the organization of two companies. One, the Charles Ponzi Steamship Company, which would have owned the fleet. The other, the International Shipping & Mercantile Company, which would have leased and operated the vessels. The C. P. S. S. Co. was to be capitalized at $1,000,000, or 1,000 shares of common stock at $1,000 each. This company would have issued $350,000,000 of 12% ten-year bonds.

The I. S. & M. Co. would have been capitalized at $350,000,000, with 3,500,000 shares of 8% ten-year preferred stock, and 7,000,000 shares of no-par-value common.

The I. S. & M. Co. would have exchanged 3,500,000 shares of its common stock for 500 shares of the C. P. S. S. Co.'s common. Then it would have underwritten the entire bond issue at 93. Or, for

$325,500. Paying for it with demand notes. It would have offered for sale to the public at large one $100 - bond, one $100-share of preferred and one of no-par-value common for $200. Notes of the Securities Exchange Company, at their maturity value, would have been accepted in payment, in lieu of cash. The sale of the stock, whether for cash, or against such notes, would have wiped out all liabilities of the Securities Exchange Company. And that company would have passed out of existence.

The next step was to find a way to wipe out the indebtedness of the two new companies. To this end, the I. S. & M. Co. would have leased the entire fleet by paying to the C. P. S. S. Co. $80,000,000 a year for ten years. The C. P. S. S. Co. would have applied the 80 millions to the payment of interest on the bond issue and to the amortization of the principal. The interest would have amounted to 420 millions in ten years. The 38 millions set aside each year for the amortization of the principal, would have earned easily 3% net. Or not less than 12 millions in ten years. Leaving $42,000,000 after payment of the principal, to be distributed as dividend to the common stock. Something like $42,000 a share!

The I. S. & M. Co. would have sub-leased the vessels to a number of subsidiary companies for 150 million dollars a year for ten years. That would have left the company $70.000,000 a year with which to pay the interest on its preferred stock and for the amortization of the principal. The interest would have amounted to 280 millions in ten years. The 43 millions set aside each year for the amortization of the principal would have earned 3%. Or. not less than $15,000,000 in ten years. Leaving 85 millions, after payment of the principal, to be distributed as dividend to the common stock. About 12 dollars a share.

At the end of ten years, it did not matter, so far as I was concerned, what became of the fleet, from the standpoint of money. It would have earned for me and my companies everything I had planned it should earn. But, in order that my ten-year plan might be successful, I would have to organize and control a number of subsidiary companies.

Such companies would have been capitalized in accordance with their requirements. Their capitalization would have consisted of preferred stock and no-par-value common. The I. S. & M. Co. would have retained 51% of all the common in each instance. The preferred and the remaining 49% of the common would have been offered to manufacturers, exporters, , and importers. Some, to the general public. Each subsidiary company would have paid to the I. S. & M. Co. a rental price of $15 per dead-weight ton per year for such vessels as it might have leased.

My figures were all based on dead-weight tonnage. The' entire fleet consisted of 10,000,000 tons. Leased by the C. P. S. S. Co: to the I. S. & M. Co. for $8 a ton per year. Subleased by the I. S. & M. Co. to the subsidiary companies for $15 a ton per year.

Thus, as an illustration, a ten-thousand-ton vessel would have cost the subsidiary company $150,000 a year. In addition to the operating expenses, which I had no means of estimating. But such vessel could have made easily four round trips a year. Even to distant ports. And could have carried, therefore, 80,000 tons of cargo.

Assuming that the operating expenses amounted to $8 per ton, still it would have cost them altogether only $10 a ton for their freight. And that was about one-half of what shippers were paying in those days.

Each subsidiary company would have operated its own vessels independently. The freight boats, I mean. Insofar as it was practical to do so. Insofar as it could guarantee a full cargo both ways. The I. S. & M. Co. would have operated all of such other vessels as the subsidiary companies could not themselves operate. In that case, the actual operating expenses, plus the lease price per ton, would have been prorated on the basis of the freight-tonnage carried.

It was also my plan that passenger steamers should be used as floating sample rooms for American products. They would travel from port to port, carrying those tourists who might care to go along. But carrying particularly American salesmen and buyers, a variety of samples, and a whole cargo of goods. Goods that could be delivered right from the boat to any chance foreign buyer. On their return trips, those boats would have picked up whatever freight they could, or goods especially bought right on the spot by the American buyers on board.

Apparently, the whole scheme was a money-making proposition. I was optimistic enough to believe that I would have cleaned up several millions. Not only that, but I believed also that I had discovered a safe way out of my difficulties. However, I was only secondarily interested in the profitable aspect of the thing. Primarily, it was my object to restore the prestige of the American Merchant Marine.

I was a patriotic cuss in those days. American in everything, except in name, because my full papers were not due yet. One hundred per cent American. More so than many natives. Including those in Wall Street and in Washington who were doing their darndest to keep the American boats rotting at anchor, in order that the International Mercantile Marine of John Bull might not lose its supremacy.

Nothing would have pleased me more than to see the Stars and Stripes float where the Union Jack was then floating. With every blessed thing any country might wish for, in the way of products and money, and plenty of both, I could not see the sense for the United States of having to depend on foreign shipping. And nobody in America could see any sense, either. Except those who were responsible for the situation. But if they saw any sense in it, it must have been spelled c-e-n-t-s. And it must have summed up to a good many dollars. Pardon my error, I should have said pounds sterling. Of the same coinage in which Benedict Arnold was paid.

CHAPTER XXIV

MR. PONZI IS FIFTEEN MILLION BUCKS AHEAD OF GAME, BUT DOES NOT QUIT

My mind was made up to buy the Shipping Board fleet. Failing that, I was determined to buy up banks, right and left. In either event, I needed all the money I could lay my hands on. Receipts of $1,000,000 a day were not enough. They were like a drop in the bucket. I needed more. And the only way to get it, was to go after it by opening more offices.

At that time, I had about 180 agents and sub-agents in New England. But only 35 offices. With the result that some of the offices had from half a dozen to a dozen sub-agents. In Greater Boston, all of my 50 or more agents and sub-agents dealt with my office in School Street. They were in and out all day long. And they would send their customers.

Things got so bad that I had to do something to relieve the congestion. I couldn't cope with it. Not even with the ten or twelve cops I had hired to regulate the traffic in the street and along the corridors. The jam beggars description! It's unbelievable! Only those who have seen it can believe it. Combining the two objects, i.e.. of raising money and clearing my office, I directed each of the 50 Boston agents and sub-agents to open a branch office in some district of Greater Boston. That served to divert part of the crowd rendering the situation easier to handle and at the same time bringing in more money.

Then I turned to the banks. I had already built up some large balances in several of them. For instance, $1,500,000 in the Lawrence Trust Company of Lawrence; $150,000 in the Lexington Trust Company of Lexington; $900,000 in the Merchants National Bank of Manchester, N. H.; $500,000 in the Citizens National Bank of Woonsocket, R. I.;

and any number under $100,000 but over $50,000, in smaller institutions. With the ones named, I was about ready to spring the same surprise I had sprung on the officials of the Hanover Trust Company.

That is, pay a call. Offer to buy a controlling interest. Immediately withdraw my balance, in case of refusal. All banks in general were beginning to feel the effects of heavy withdrawals. The contest I had promoted to boost the Hanover's deposits, had rendered the crisis even more acute. But it wasn't acute enough to suit me. And so, I proceeded to give them another wallop.

In the course of a meeting of the executive committee of the Hanover Trust, it struck me that bank depositors in general were not receiving a square deal. They were at the mercy of the board of directors who might and might not be honest men. Some of them are not. They are burglars. The depositors, it seemed to me, were not receiving adequate returns for the risks they were incurring.

As these thoughts were flashing through my mind, I was paying very little attention to the meeting, but a good deal to a new plan of banking reform. So, before the meeting came to a close, I arose and addressed the members.

"Gentlemen," I said, "I desire to submit a suggestion to your vote. It occurs to me that this committee has supreme control over the millions which our depositors have entrusted to this bank. We may or may not exercise that control judiciously. If we do, we earn some extra stock dividends. If we don't, we might lose not over twice the amount of our holdings, or $800,000 while our depositors may lose several millions. The greater risk is theirs. Theirs is the greater loss. Yet, when all goes well, we only pay them about 4% a year. The situation seems unfair. I would be in favor of extending to depositors greater privileges and larger returns. For instance, I suggest that the depositors be permitted to-elect a certain number of directors. They have a right to know what is being done at these meetings. In addition, I suggest that stockholders be paid a definite dividend of 7%, the same as the depositors are being paid 4%. All net earnings in excess of that should be equally prorated between stockholders and depositors. In other words, I advocate profit sharing banking. I fully realized that my doctrines may appear almost revolutionary, but I am sure they are equitable and fair, I desire your vote on the following questions. First, shall the Hanover Trust Company take the initiative in advocating such a reform, and second, shall Ponzi be permitted to inform the newspapers about the suggestions submitted at this meeting ?"

The committee voted both questions in the affirmative and I departed to consult my counsel who had supervision over my banking activities. We decided to invite the financial editors of every Boston paper to a meeting and we arranged for a room at Young's Hotel. 'They came, and I put the proposition up to them. But I could read in their countenances that they would never dare to throw that monkey wrench into the Boston banking machinery. They knew only too well which side of their bread was buttered. In fact, the next day they reported that, after consultation with their managing editors, they couldn't publicly endorse my plan.

"All right, boys," I told them, "I can still obtain publicity without your papers. I shall organize a publicity bureau and circularize every bank depositor in New England."

"It' will cost you some money,"' one of them remarked.

"Money? What's money to me? Money means nothing to me," I replied. "I would give a million any day for a good cause."

The following day, at the suggestion of my counsel and the bank officers, I hired a publicity manager, and the moment I hired him I gave my counsel $7,000 to rent suitable offices for a publicity bureau, and to cover incidental expenses.

Under my publicity manager's direction, I was going to circularize every bank depositor in New England, explaining my profit sharing plan. Anybody can realize what that would have meant. Any bank that would have gone on record against such a plan would have been boycotted. It would have had to contend with runs, and since no bank was in a position to cope with a run for over 48 hours, it would have had to go under, or sell out to me.

While my publicity manager and counsel were, presumably, carrying out my instructions, my attention was engaged by the activities of an outfit called the Old Colony Foreign Exchange Company. It was made up of a few fellows who had failed to land a job with me. That Company professed to be doing exactly what I was doing, and everybody believed them, because everybody believed that I was doing the right thing.

I couldn't come out and say that the other fellow was lying, just like I was. They had me by the small of the neck, and the best that I could do was to squirm. They went so far as to have notes printed exactly like mine, except for the company's name, to which the average investor paid no attention. In fact, most of the people who invested with the Old Colony thought that they were investing with me. From the standpoint of inroads in my cash receipts, they were not doing much damage. But what was bothering me was the danger that the authorities might take some action against them. None of them had either the courage or the ability to hold their own in a match of wits. They would have been exposed in no time, and if they had been exposed it would have been almost impossible for me to have escaped the same fate.

I sent word for them to cut it out and I threatened them but it did not do any good. They defied me; not because they were brave, but because they were fools. They even went and hired an office on the same floor as mine and then they started to divert my own investors from my office to their own company by claiming that we were one and the same company.

I got tired of that racket and decided to give them a lesson, even if I had to swing for it. I called in the Pinkertons and put them on the trail of every man and woman connected with the Old Colony Foreign Exchange Company.

"Find out all that you can about them," were my instructions to Murray, the Pinkerton's Boston Manager.

"Follow them everywhere; to China, if necessary. Never lose sight of any of them, day or night, and send me a daily report and a copy to District Attorney Pelletier. Spare no expense. I want you to land those people in jail."

I couldn't let them get away with what they were doing. They constituted for me a greater menace than all of the government agencies put together. Perhaps my activities were not entirely within the law. They were as objectionable. But my intent was honest. I was in a critical position and I had fallen into it without any intention to do wrong. Now that I was in it I was trying my hardest to pull myself out of it, without hurting my investors. The means I was resorting to, in order to swim out of the hole, might not have been sound and might not have been entirely legitimate, but I felt that the end justified the means, and the end, my purpose, was not dishonest. For that reason I could not tolerate that outfit. I could not let them stand in the way of my investors and my own welfare.

Leaving the Pinkertons to take care of the Old Colony gang, I conferred with my publicity manager and my counsel. According to what they said, the organization of the publicity bureau was progressing satisfactorily. Like the patient who registers a temperature of 105 in the shade. He is always "progressing satisfactorily". If you believe the nurse. But in the wrong direction. And nobody knows differently until after he's dead.

I took it for granted that my instructions were being carried out. Or soon would be. And I accepted McMasters' suggestion that some newspaper publicity would help things along. I actually commended him for it. And when he told me that the Boston Post had agreed to feature the Securities Exchange Company and myself, I was tickled to death.

On July 24, 1920, the Boston Post published the promised article. The 24th was a Saturday. A day when all business usually stops at noon. A day when almost everybody ducks the city for the country or the beaches. But it wasn't on that particular Saturday. It seemed, instead, as if everybody had made a date to meet at 27 School Street! Everybody was there. The 2,000,000 inhabitants of Greater Boston were all there! If there were not exactly 2,000,000 they looked that many.

The day after, Sunday, the Boston Post found it could spare even more room for Ponzi. So, it gave me a couple of pages. The Herald, The Globe, The Advertiser, could not let the Post get away with a scoop like that. They too jumped into the fray. With front page stuff. And they covered me and the Securities Exchange Company from head to foot. Like a blanket. I never realized what a big fellow I was, until after I had read all of the papers.

That Sunday was no day of rest for me. Telegram and telephone calls began to pour into my house at daybreak. From everybody. Big men and little men. Every one of them anxious to get on the right side of me. Because I was a multimillionaire. I received more congratulations than a President elect! More persons called at my residence in a day than are usually seen at the Brockton Fair in three days! More automobiles went by my house than Ford and General Motors can put out in six months! I had to give out more interviews and pose for more pictures than a movie star of the first magnitude. All summed up, that Sunday was the busiest day in all my life I ever put in doing nothing!

But both that Saturday and that Sunday were mild compared with the Monday that followed them! The newspapers had not let up. They were still pouring kerosene on the blaze. And when I got down to School

Street, the conditions I found beggar description.

All vehicle traffic had been suspended. My and Mayor Peters' car were the only two permitted to navigate School Street. "Navigate" is right. The whole street was a sea of straw hats and squirming humanity! In front of the Niles Building, six mounted policemen were on duty, regulating the crowd. Fourteen or more uniformed officers were doing duty inside of the building. A huge line of investors, four abreast, stretched from the City Hall Annex, through City Hill Avenue and School Street, to the entrance of the Niles Building, up stairways, along the corridors ... all the way to my office!

The air was tense with ill suppressed excitement. Hope and greed could be read in everybody's countenance. Guessed from the wads of money nervously clutched and waved by thousands of outstretched fists! Madness, money madness, the worst kind of madness, was reflected in everybody's eyes! In a silent exhibition of utter disdain to all principles of calm and careful judgment. In a silent exhibition of reckless mob psychology, entirely too susceptible to the fatal spell of misguided or perverted leadership!

The scene deployed before me, as I alighted from my car, is something that no man could forget. To the crowd there assembled, I was the realization of their dreams. The idol. The hero. The master and arbiter of their lives. Of their hopes. Of their fortunes. The discoverer of wealth and happiness. The "wizard" who could turn a pauper into a millionaire overnight!

That scene spelled success for me. It couldn't spell anything else. The crowd in School Street was fairly represents five of the millions of men and women who were ready to do exactly the same thing. Ready to invest with me. To give me their money. All they had. As soon as I made it possible for them to get to me. Nothing could stand in the way of the most complete achievement of my ambitions. I had won!

On that Monday morning, my cash receipts reached their peak. In my School Street office alone, I took in one million dollars in three hours. More than all of the Boston banks put together had taken in during the same three hours. I don't know how much my other offices took in. But the rush of investors was general in every community where I had an office. Their legion was in excess of 30,000. The combined face value of the Securities Exchange Company's notes they held, was $15,000,000! New England had come through in grand style! The Yan kees and the Puritans were no pikers! They had bought my six-cent international reply coupon for $15,000,000! just as I thought they would! Even if they never got anything for it, it was cheap at that price. Without malice aforethought, I had given them the best show that was ever staged in their territory since the landing of the Pilgrims! I had given them the most brazen exhibition of sheer nerve that had ever been witnessed in the world of finance! I had given them the longest ride, the most mileage, for their money they had ever got before or since! It was easily worth fifteen million bucks to watch me put the thing over!

CHAPTER XXV

THE BATTLE ROYAL IS ON, WITH THE ODDS IN FAVOR OF MR. PONZI

The international reply coupon I had set out to sell was sold. And how! There was no doubt as to that. Not only was it sold, but I had got a fairly good price for it too. Fifteen million bucks for a six-cent item are not to be sneezed at anywhere. Not even in New England where the average dollar is trained from infancy to breed faster than a guinea pig. However, my day's work was not over yet. Not by a long shot. Because I had to see to it that the coupon might stay sold. And the indications were that it wouldn't.

In fact the outlook was far from favorable. It might have looked rosy to me, for a moment. From the time I alighted from my car and went upstairs to my office, until I emerged again, ten or fifteen minutes later, to go to the Hanover Trust. But after I had a chance to peruse the morning papers, and especially the Boston Post, in the privacy of the bank president's office, it came home to me that the situation was considerably more tense than it had ever been.

The press was unanimous in its condemnation of official laxity. My activities were not openly qualified as fraudulent. Because the newspapers knew better. But they were pictured so far out of the ordinary, magnified to such an extent, as to make them appear absurd. And the officials were blamed for having failed to check up properly the various claims upon which my activities were based.

The situation was especially dangerous because a man in public office generally runs amuck the moment he becomes the target of printed criticism. Under the spur of what he believes to be a public opinion, he is apt to do almost anything. Except keep quiet. He will not hesitate to misuse his authority. To misconstrue the law. To lapse from blunder to perfidy. Rather than to come right out like a man and explain that his failure to act is due to circumstances over which he has no control.

After I read the papers, I began to fear just that. Within the day, within the next hour or so, some proceedings might be instituted against me. Whether civil or criminal, I didn't know. But proceedings which might have closed me down. Justly or unjustly. Temporarily, or for good. Such as an injunction.

Without any doubt, I had a battle on my hands. This time with the press, in general.

I reached for the phone.

"Call up the United States Attorney, and District Attorney," I directed the Hanover's switch-board operator, "and tell them I want to talk to them. Give me the calls as they come in."

The United States Attorney was the first one to answer.

"I assume you have read the papers," I told him.

"I have," he admitted.

"It occurs to me," I continued, "that it is rather unfair for them to criticize public officials for their alleged laxity. Personally, I resent the criticism because of its implications. I am going to demand a show-down. I am going to offer you and the other officials an opportunity to investigate my business. Would you be willing to join the attorney-general and district attorney at a conference with me, in order that the details of such investigation may be arranged?"

The Assistant U. S. District Attorney replied that he would be glad to. Mr. District Attorney sent word for me to go over to his office and he would talk to me. Attorney-General said that a joint conference was not agreeable to him.

"But, Mr. Attorney-General," I argued, "I'm a busy man. I can't spend a whole day in conferences. I feel that the consideration I am showing to the authorities should meet with equal consideration from them. After all, you must realize that, under the law, no investigation can take place without my consent."

It was a waste of time to argue with him. I couldn't move him. And I was on the verge of telling him to go to the devil. But as yet, I didn't know him well enough for that. And so, I agreed to go up to his office later in the day.

"About what time?" he asked me.

"I couldn't say," I replied. "As soon as I get through with the state and federal officials."

"I'll be waiting for you," he said, but he did not know how long I was going to keep him waiting. Since he wanted to be so disagreeable, I intended to make him whistle. And if he didn't know how, he could learn.

The phone calls disposed of, I had to do some quick thinking. I stood committed to an investigation. And had to go through with it. I wouldn't and couldn't go back on my word. But it was vital for me to decide upon the type of investigation which might satisfy the officials and the public without disclosing my true situation. By a process of elimination, I arrived at something that looked pretty good.

Acting on the impulse, as usual, I went to the Court House to put my proposition up to Mr. District Attorney. I had never met him before. I did not know what sort of a fellow he was. But I found him none too pleasant at the start.

"It is being rumored," he said, "that I have $20,000 invested with you. Under the circumstances, I feel that I ought to investigate the sort of business in which my money is supposed to be invested."

"That's right," I agreed with him, "as an investor it would be your privilege to investigate. At the proper time. That is, before investing. But it so happens that you are not an investor of record. Therefore, it does not seem that you have any interest in the matter."

"I have," he stated. "I am the District Attorney of Suffolk County and, as such, I owe to my constituents the protection of this office in anything that may affect their welfare."

"But there is no indication that the welfare of your constituents is being jeopardized," I argued. "You have no complaints upon which to base any action."

"That's true," he admitted, "but the newspapers are openly hinting that you are perpetrating a fraud upon the public."

"If I am," I remarked, "it seems to me that you should welcome my call, because I have come to offer you an opportunity to investigate my activities."

"Do you mean it?" he asked.

"Certainly," I said. "I wouldn't be here, if I didn't. If I didn't intend to cooperate with you, I would let you take the first step while I would hire half a dozen of the best lawyers to resist your investigations."

"If that is the case," he stated, "I am ready to listen to you with an open mind. What have you got to offer?"

"An opportunity to ascertain whether or not I am solvent." I replied. "What the authorities are interested to know at this time is whether or not I have enough money to meet all of my outstanding notes."

"How do you propose to show that?" he asked.

"By allowing an auditor, acceptable to all of the officials concerned, to determine the total of my liabilities," I explained.

"Will you let that auditor examine your books?" he went on."

"I will turn over to him all of the books, papers and records which are necessary to determine my liabilities," I stated. "And no more."

"How is he going to verify whether or not you are solvent?" he inquired.

"I will attend to that," I replied. "When the total of my liabilities will be announced, I shall exhibit my assets. Is that satisfactory?"

"Yes," he said," "but who is going to pick out the auditor?"

"You and the other officials," I told him. "I don't care who the auditor is. Only, I want it understood that there is going to be one investigation for all of the officials concerned. And not a separate investigation for each one of them."

"Why do you say that?" he asked.

"Because, from my phone conversation with the Attorney General, I have reason to believe that he wants to conduct a separate investigation of his own," I replied.

"For my part," said Mr. District Attorney, "I am willing to agree to a joint investigation."

"And so is the Assistant United States District Attorney," I stated. "Therefore, unless the Attorney General falls in with the majority, he'll be out of luck. That's all there is to it." It was at this point that I felt the psychological moment had arrived for an announcement intended to upset my opponents.

"Mr. District Attorney," I said, "it occurs to me just now that it might be an impossible task for an auditor to determine my liabilities, if I should continue to issue notes every day throughout the investigation."

"I guess it would be at that," he agreed. "Couldn't you stop issuing those notes?"

"I could," I admitted, "but I haven't had the time to consider whether it would be expedient for me, to do so. However, the suggestion has an appealing feature. Because it offers me the opportunity to spike certain insinuations which are being made by the press, I will do it."

"You will stop issuing notes?" he asked. "When?"

"Right now," I told him. "May I use your phone?"

"Surely," he said. "Help yourself."

I called up my office. Miss Meli answered.

"Miss Meli," I directed her, "from this moment we shall cease accepting money for investment. Until further order. Post a couple of notices around the office. Notify by phone or wire all agents and sub-agents. But we shall continue to redeem notes as usual. At maturity, with interest. Before maturity, without it."

"Mr. Ponzi," said the District Attorney after I had replaced the receiver, "I had probably misjudged you before you entered this office. Your frankness impresses me favorably. I believe you mean to do the right thing. I want to thank you for facilitating my task and I want also to assure you that I will not put you to any greater inconvenience than is absolutely necessary."

From his office, I went to call on the United States Attorney. I related to him what had occurred. And he seemed entirely satisfied with it. He said he would consult with the District Attorney and let we know later about the auditor.

I left the office of the Assistant United States District Attorney to go to the State House where the Attorney General had been waiting for me for the last three or four hours. But, on my way, I had to drop in at my office to straighten things out. My announcement that I would not accept any more money, had provoked a run. I found as many investors ready to withdraw their money, as I had seen there in the morning eager to give it to me. Only, the cops were missing and the crowd was not as orderly.

I entered my office and was told that the police on duty had been recalled. Immediately, I phoned to the Police Commissioner. I couldn't get him.

Finally, I got the Superintendent on the wire. He said that the police had been withdrawn because it was against the law for them to be on duty in private buildings.

"That's a fine time to tell me!" I exploded. "So long as I was taking in money and presumably, stealing it and committing a felony, it was all right for the police to protect me. Now that I am performing a lawful act, that of making restitution, the law denies me protection There is something fishy somewhere, but I haven't the time to bother with you fellows. You can tell the Commissioner I don't need his police force. I will organize one of my own."

And I did. I hired the Pinkertons and other private guards. Inside of an hour I had the crowd under control. Without resorting to violence. I went personally through the line of investors. Talking to them. Explaining things. Making it easy for them to get their money. And with that I averted another vicious blow.

The police, as I was told later, had been withdrawn in the hope that some rioting might develop and furnish a pretext to the authorities to step in and take charge. I don't know for sure where the order came from. I learned, however, that political and financial interests had caused that order to be issued. But I disappointed them. As soon as I had things running smoothly in my office, I went to call on the Attorney General.

I brought a lawyer along with me as a precaution. I had the intuition that I wasn't going to a mere conference. In fact, when I entered the Attorney General's office, I found about a dozen people sitting at a long table. Assistant A. Gs. galore. Stenographers. And what not. The only one missing was the official executioner.

Fortunately, there wasn't what you may call a keen intellect in the whole bunch.

The conference wasn't much of an ordeal. Except from the standpoint of time. It lasted longer than any other. Because my audience was just naturally slower. At grasping things. But, on the other hand, I got away with more fibs. Some of them actually awful. And had the pleasure of leaving that distinguished gathering as much in the dark about my activities as they were at the start. Only, they didn't realize it. Ignorance is bliss.

On my way home, in the evening, I had twenty or thirty minutes in which to review the events of the day. So far, I was still master of the situation. The Assistant United States District Attorney had appointed Edwin L. Pride, a noted accountant, to compile the list of my liabilities. The District Attorney had declared himself ready to abide by Prides findings. The Attorney General had been left out in the cold. He wasn't likely to make any trouble because, with two district attorneys on my side, he didn't have a chance either with the courts or the public.

But, even if I was still master of the situation, the fact remained that I did not have enough money or assets to balance my liabilities. Nobody knew that except myself. Yet, it looked as if the whole world would know it before long. Unless … That's it! Unless I happened to have a couple of wild deuces up my sleeve. And I had them all right. I had tucked them there myself in the morning.

In fact, for one thing, I had nothing to fear and everything to gain from the run I had provoked. I had enough liquid cash to keep on paying out half a million a day for two weeks. The chances were that I would have paid out an average of half that amount per day. For four weeks, instead of two. Then, in a pinch, I could have liquidated my other assets and stretched things along for another week. But the best feature of the run was that I would have redeemed more notes without interest than with interest. Because frightened investors would not have waited for their notes to mature. Even a few days. And every time I refunded the principal, I would save the 50% interest.

Roughly, I owed then $15,000,000. Of which $5,000,000. were interest. My total resources were around $8,000,000. And I was $7,000,000 in the hole. But, by refunding the principal only, before maturity, instead of paying principal and interest, at maturity, with $8,000,000 I would have wiped out $12,000,000 of liabilities. And made a gain of $4,000,000. True enough, I would still be in a hole $3,000,000. But the second wild deuce would have taken care of that.

The second deuce was the Hanover Trust Company. The bank had, at that time, easily $5,000,000 in negotiable securities and plenty of liquid cash. They were not mine. They were the bank's. But I had access to them.

Now, the Hanover was located at the corner of Washington and

Water Streets. The United States Attorney's office was at the corner of Devonshire and Water Streets. The two were less than one-half block apart. My plan was to have the showdown in the office of the Assistant United States District Attorney. As soon as he was ready to announce the total of my liabilities, I would have gone up to his office with all of the cancelled notes, all of my bank books, and all of my other assets, whether in the form of deeds or stocks. But, on my way over, I would have dropped in at the Hanover and grabbed enough securities and cash to make up the difference between the liabilities and my actual assets. The show-down might have lasted an hour or so. On the way back, I would have replaced in the Hanover what I had temporarily taken away. And nobody would have known the difference.

The investigation would have ended right there and then. The authorities would have to certify as to my solvency. And I would have resumed my activities with an officially clean bill of health.

All considered, I was far from licked yet. But I certainly had to be on the alert twenty-four hours of the day. For the next two or three weeks. The banks, the authorities and the press were all after my scalp.

CHAPTER XXVI

OH, BOY! WHAT A FIGHT! THE FUR IS STILL FLYING AND YOU CAN'T TELL WHICH IS WHICH!

The next day brought new excitement in the form of a petition for an injunction filed by an attorney, for one of my investors who held one of my notes for $500. Neither he nor his claim had a leg to stand on, between the two.

I scouted for the creditor all over Boston. To settle his claim. Even if I had to give ten times what I owed him. But he could not be found. Neither could I reach his attorney. So, I told Sam Bailen, one of my several lawyers, to appear and oppose the petition.

In the meanwhile, I made arrangements to retain Dan Coakley. I needed a man of his caliber to cope with the State House crowd.

Still, my hiring of Dan Coakley was a blunder. A political blunder. Some officials had no use for Dan. Dan, a firm believer in reciprocity, had no use for them. Which made it mutual. In so far as they were concerned. But raised hell with my peaceful progress, in so far as I was concerned. It placed me, so to speak, between the devil and the deep blue sea. And it was a toss up which one was the devil.

The moment Dan stepped into the picture, some officials made up their mind to take out on me what they couldn't take out on Dan. And I became the pliant pig-skin, the football, in the game between the two teams. For which I got more kicks in the slats than any man alive. It's a wonder that I can still sit down without wincing.

What I should have done, instead of hiring Dan, was to stroll down to State Street and pick me out one of those lawyers with a Mayflower pedigree. One of those blue-ribbon Pomeranians. Or Spaniels. With an appetite like a Great Dane. Or a Saint Bernard. Then, I could have got away with murder. Or, with millions, rather. One of my contemporaries wasn't a sap like me. He went and hired for himself some real aristocratic counsel. It might have cost him part of his fortune. But not his liberty. Like it did me.

Anyway, blunder or no blunder, I am not sorry I hired Dan Coakley. Even if I got in Dutch with the highbrows. It was worth all I went through, to meet Dan. To have his friendship. The benefit of his advice. The most competent advice in the State of Massachusetts. Bar none. To watch his brilliant mind at work. And to fight alongside of him. Against the same outfit. The same bunch of professional buccaneers whose only title to respectability rests in the fact that they are in power. That they sit pretty. Because they are subservient to the money interests.

I put in the best part of that day straightening out that customer's business. I was still searching for him and had almost given up all hope to find him, when he walked right into my office. He was upset and indignant. He had seen his name on the bulletin board of a Boston newspaper and he didn't know what it was all about. I explained the situation to him and he claimed that he bad been misled into signing that petition. I rushed up to my attorney's office and made the customer sign an affidavit. Less than an hour later, his attorney withdrew the petition.

The run was progressing satisfactorily for a run. The crowd was orderly. Checks were being issued at the rate of about 200 per hour. Brother Pride was busy listing my liabilities from the note stubs I had turned over to him. Out of-town bank accounts were being gradually reduced and the money concentrated into the Hanover Trust. There was a reason for that. By paying my depositors with checks drawn on that Bank they would have to go there to cash them. Many might feel inclined to leave the money there and open an account, and that is just exactly what did happen. Most of the money I paid out of one pocket was re-deposited in the other. It was a case of "heads I win" and "tails you lose."

The city editor of one of the Boston newspapers was still at it; that is, still dogging my footsteps, only a little more cautiously, but not less persistently. Never letting me out of his sight and nothing less than a shower of buckshot would have discouraged him, and I was just wishing that he was a "deer" instead of being a "dear." Just then my attention was diverted by one of his confreres, the publisher of a local financial sheet. That he, of all men, would come out and call me names was something I couldn't swallow.

Out of a clear sky he gave me more display on his sheet than he ordinarily would have given to one of his friends; the stock-exchange paper hangers, even at one hundred bucks an inch. What he didn't say about me wasn't fit to be printed, no more than what I thought about him was. And he did not spare me, only he forgot to hire a lawyer as a proofreaders with the result that he left himself wide open and I flew at him. I sued him for $5,000,000. He had a dairy farm near-by and I attached everything he had. I tied him up so thoroughly, that the morning after the attachment even his cows couldn't give milk.

About that time, a telegram from New York came to liven things up a bit. As if they weren't lively enough. The telegram informed me that a certain Joseph Hermann "of London and Melbourne" was on his way to Boston to confer with me on an important deal. A little later I got a phone call informing me of his arrival, and I arranged to meet him at the Parker House.

The interview was brief. He said he represented some New York and Paris capitalists. And had come to purchase, if possible, the Securities Exchange Company. His statement found we quite unreceptive. I did not believe he meant business. However, I talked things over with him. just to see what his game was.

"Are you familiar with the conditions of the Securities Exchange Company?" I asked him.

"Only to the extent described by the newspapers," he said.

"Well, then, let me inform you," I suggested. "All of the company's assets consist of cash. Its liabilities are represented by notes. When I shall have redeemed my last note all of the left over cash will be my own property. The company will have a fairly good supply of office furniture, fixtures, equipment and a wonderful mailing list. Are you prepared to buy that?"

"Yes," he admitted, "that's just exactly what we want."

"All right, then," I said. "We will not bother to figure out the furniture, fixtures and equipment. I will throw all of that in, for good measure.

But we must agree upon the price you shall pay me for the mailing list and the good will."

"We shall leave it to you to name your figure," he stated. "We shall endeavor to meet your terms."

He acted too blamed optimistic to sound convincing. I had a feeling he was bluffing. So, I decided to name an exorbitant figure. Which would have forced him to show his hand.

"I want ten million dollars," I told him.

"It is a large sum," he commented, "but we are prepared to produce it. Personally, I accept your figure. However, I must return to New York to consult with my associates. We will all be here the day after tomorrow to discuss the details. Will it be convenient for you to meet us on that day at the Copley Plaza between 9 and 10 A. M.?"

"Yes, I'll be there," I agreed. "But please remember that my price is for cash on delivery. Subject to increase, if you cause me to lose my time unnecessarily."

At the appointed date, we met again. We discussed the matter for almost two hours. By then I had learned that they were fully supplied with funds. There was even a rumor current that they were backed by one of the largest banking houses in America. A rumor which I was never able to verify. But I had grown suspicious of their purpose. So, I altered my terms.

"I do not know what you propose to do with my company," I told them. "I assume that you want to use it to further some enterprise of your own. I could turn it over to you and give you a free hand. Without worrying what may happen afterwards. But I feel morally obligated toward my investors and the public to protect them against dangerous investment. So, I will sell out only to persons who will not use the company for illegitimate purposes. I don't know any of you gentlemen. Even if I did, I would not assume the responsibility of endorsing you. Therefore, I will sell to you on the condition that you will give me an executive position in your company. I don't want any salary. I ask for no share of the profits. All I want is the most ample opportunity of keeping a check on what you are doing. After I shall have satisfied myself in that respect, I will withdraw."

"We are willing to agree to that," Hermann sad for him and the others.

Regardless of the obstacles I created, I simply couldn't discourage those men. However, they were not ready to close the deal that day. And suggested a new conference.

"I don't see any necessity for further conferences,'" I stated. "You know my terms. Have a regular contract drawn up by your attorneys and bring it to me for my signature. We can close the deal in fifteen minutes. I cannot see you again until you are ready to close the deal. When you are, you shall exhibit to me a certified check for ten million dollars before I even consent to talk to you. I am too busy right now to spend any more time in this sort of conference."

The Hermann's visits could have been my salvation. If I had had sense enough to take advantage of them. Without developing a conscience. Which was never appreciated either then or since. But my mind was running along the wrong channels at that time. I had more live preservers thrown at me than a ship-wreck. Yet I was so wrapped up in those crazy notions of mine that I never so much as reached for one.

I felt so sure of myself that I never looked ahead further than my nose. Big and little politicians were trailing me right along. And I didn't have to go looking for overtures. They were being made right to me.

For instance, one morning a couple of politicians called at my residence before breakfast. One of them was a representative of a New York newspaper. I received him in the sun-parlor in my pajamas.

"Mr. Ponzi, here are our credentials," said he, handing me some letters which showed his connection with the Republican National Committee. "We are sent by one of its leaders and the National Committee of the Republican Party to solicit your contribution to the campaign. We have been told of your success and liberality and have taken the liberty to hope that you will contribute."

"You may have come to the right church," I replied to him, "but I believe you have stepped into the wrong pew."

"Why?" be asked. "You certainly appreciate the fact that Senator Harding will be the next President of the United States?"

"Perhaps," I remarked. "Unless Cox beats him to it."

"Not a chance," he said. "The Democrats are due for defeat!"

"Well, how much do you expect from me?" I inquired.

"Anything you care to give," he answered. "In your position, you would hardly contribute less than a thousand dollars, I believe."

"Is that all you want?" I asked. "Why, a thousand dollars is no money at all. I thought you said I was liberal."

"Of course," he said. "You can give as much as you like and we can assure you that the more you will give us the more we shall be pleased."

"If I were to follow my inclinations I would contribute considerably more than a thousand dollars," I told him.

"We are glad to hear it." he acknowledged. "How much will you say?"

"How much will I say?" I repeated after him. "I will say a cool million, in round figures."

"A million dollars?" he asked with amazement.

"Yes," I confirmed. "A whole million dollars, gentlemen, ... to hang the whole Republican Party!"

"Evidently your language indicates that you have some grievances against our party," said he.

"Grievances? That's no word for it!" I told him. "While you are here soliciting my contribution, look at what they are doing to ruin me. They are all Republicans. Wouldn't I be a sap to contribute to their political success while they are actually conspiring against me?"

"We didn't know that," he apologized.

"Inform yourselves. then," I suggested. "Go and tell your friends to lay off. And then come and talk to me about contributions. But not before."

"We will see what we can do," he said. "Will you make an appointment to see us later?"

"I will not make any appointment now," I told him, "but you can have a talk with judge Leveroni. If you reach a satisfactory arrangement, I will accept his recommendations."

Once more I had turned the cold shoulder on the team. The winning team. In some way or another, I always managed to place my bets on the wrong horse. For a gambler, I certainly was a corker!

CHAPTER XXVII

A COUPLE OF WINDJAMMERS SETTLE MR. PONZI'S GOOSE AND HE G0ES DOWN FOR THE COUNT OF TEN

Toward the end of the first week of the run, my payments had dwindled down to a few thousand dollars per day. My investors had made up their mind to hold their notes until maturity. And earn their 50%. The editor of one of the Boston papers was at his wits' end. For the first time in his life, he had found himself up against a surprise. A "banker" who could weather a run. And he did not know what to make of it.

However, he had gone too far to give up the fight. He spent a busy weekend, preparing for a new offensive. And recruiting some allies. Among them, one Chiaramonte. Chiaramonte knew me from Montreal. And brought to him the information that I had done time in Canada.

Monday morning, August 2nd, that newspaper carried a huge headline. "PONZI HOPELESSLY INSOLVENT," it read. Which contained many inaccurate statements. And some utterly false. That blow was a whopper! If it didn't knock me cold, it's a wonder. But it certainly raised the deuce! The run blazed out with new vigor. And for the next two or three days I paid out close to two millions.

But the run wasn't the only thing I had to contend with. I was being double crossed on all sides. One of my help saw his opportunity and took advantage. of it. He issued notes by using straw names and managed to file the stubs with the rest of them. Then he gave the notes to some of his friends and had them presented for payment. All my clerks could do was to compare them with the stubs. We had no means of knowing whether or not we had ever received the money. So, we paid them. How many of them? I don't know exactly. But I estimate the defalcation at about a quarter of a million.

Beside him, other clerks robbed me of at least one hundred thousand dollars. By the simple expedient of not marking "cancelled" on notes which had already been paid, and presenting them for payment through a confederate. I have a complete record of them. As well as of other notes issued by some clerks to themselves or their relatives and paid with interest, long before maturity. They did that by juggling the date on the face of the note. A date that should have matched the cancellation date on the revenue stamps. But didn't.

The stealing wasn't serious from the standpoint that it diverted my attention from other matters. Because it didn't. I was aware of the fact that I was being robbed. But it was serious on account of the inroads it was making in my bank balance. My cash resources had been reduced considerably. By about $5,000,000, I would say. And the run was still in full swing.

It took me the best part of the second week to restore confidence among my investors. But by Friday, I had the situation again under control. And the Boston newspaper pursuing me the hardest, was up a tree once more. Except for the Canadian lead. I learned of it somehow. And I fully realized that I was in for the worst wallop yet.

The newspaper had sent one of its best men up to Montreal. It was only a question of days before the cat would be out of the bag. Exposure could not be avoided. And exposure spelled ruin. In a way. In every way, perhaps. Except in the matter of the investigation. Of proving my solvency to the satisfaction of the officials and the public. I still had confidence to come out on top at the show-down with auditor Pride. But I needed a few more days. It was vital for me to delay the exposure until after the show-down.

In order to do that, it was necessary for me to be posted as to the progress the reporter was making up in Montreal. I had ways and means of learning what was going on in the editorial rooms of that paper. Ways which permitted me to know the Ponzi's news before the paper was in the streets. But I needed more than that. I needed to know certain things even before it did. Because I didn't want it to bluff me into some damaging admission of fact. What it might know, was not really dangerous until it could prove it. And when I was sure it could prove it, I wanted to be one step ahead of it. But I did not want to take that step until and unless I had to.

I solved the problem of learning of its progress by intercepting its telegrams. Both coming and going. A copy of every incoming telegram relating to Ponzi would be delivered to me even before it was delivered to it. Outgoing telegrams would be communicated to me almost immediately. Day or night. Its office phone was also covered. How did I arrange that? Well that would be telling. And involving others. But I can say that for each communication I paid a fancy price. Even for a millionaire. Like I was. Or supposed to be.

While this was going on, one of the officials after me was showing marked hostility. In a number of ways. Getting under my skin regularly. Like a splinter. And drawing hearty curses from me. He got to be so cordially hated around my office that one of my help, the "black sheep" of the family, decided to have him "removed". To have him "taken for a ride."

Through his connections with the underworld, he sent to New York for a gunman. He agreed to pay him $15,000 for the job. The killing of the official. Which was entirely too much money. For any official. But, in so far as that official in particular was concerned, he wasn't worth the powder to blow him to Hades.

After he had the thing all arranged, this employee came to me and told me about it. Nonchalantly. He wanted me to watch the fire-works.

"What do you think I am?" I jumped at him. "A murderer? Do you think that I would stand for anything like that? Don't you dare to go ahead with it. Because, if you do, I'll deliver you myself to the police."

"But the gunman wants to go through with it now," be protested. "He wants his money."

"A fine mess you got me into," I told him.

"I thought I was doing you a favor," he apologized.

"I don't want any of that kind of favors!" I replied to him. "If that official is an obstacle to me, I can take care of him. I don't have to have him killed. I can spend half a million to discredit him. You leave those things to me. Now, you go and find that fellow and send him to me."

The go-between as he was known, was one of the old time "gang lords." He undertook to dissuade the gunman. And send him back to New York. But he charged me $4,500 for his services. For which I made him sign a regular receipt. Only, I put an arbitrary date to it so as to cover up things.

That is about the worst investment I ever made. In the opinion of many. Including myself. I actually went and paid good money to save an enemy's life. The man who hounded me unremittingly for the next years. Notwithstanding his knowledge of what I had done for him. Because, on a latter occasion, when he had me by the nape of the neck and was telling me what a dangerous person I was, I didn't miss the chance of telling him what I had done.

But I do not regret the bad investment. Even if I paid a price far in excess of what his life was worth to the community. Forty-five cents would have been more like it. But a human life is a human life. And I wouldn't have one on my conscience for any amount.

The week-end found me scouting for cash. I don't believe I had $500,000. And stocks and property amounting to another million or more.

I tried to negotiate the certificate of deposit. Everywhere. Even in New York. But I couldn't do anything with it. The big banks had passed the word around to lay off. And everybody was laying off. I thought of Tom Lawson. The only one likely to help me. He was approached. But he wouldn't' handle it. Or couldn't. I don't know which.

Things looked kind of black. I had to have money to carry me along until the auditor was ready to report. And nobody knew when he would be ready. He might have been ready in four or five days. Or in a couple of weeks. At any rate, I had to have money for the next Monday. Because the $500,000 couldn't last much over the week-end.

I consulted with the Hanover's officials. About cashing on the certificate of deposit. It was suggested that I make out 18 demand notes for $80,000 each and one for $60,000. And that I have them signed by "dummies". Employees of the bank and others. Then, by endorsing the certificate over to the Hanover as collateral, the bank could have discounted the notes and credited the amount to my account.

I did as it was suggested.

On Monday morning, August 9th, I started to draw against the proceeds from those notes. To an extent of about $450,000. Why that much? I don't remember. I probably drew against my account for much less. But some out-of-town checks, which had not been cashed as yet, might have come in. At any rate, $450,000 of the funds from the certificate of deposit were used up on Monday morning. Then, hell broke loose! From the State House. The Bank Commissioner sent down word that the transaction was in violation of the banking laws. Maybe it was. Maybe it wasn't. It surely didn't make sense. I had $1,500,000 in that bank. And the Bank Commissioner said that the law did not permit me to draw against it! If that was the law, it was strange to me! If it wasn't the law, the commissioner was decidedly wrong. No two ways about it. But we couldn't argue with him. He ordered me to cover the overdraft immediately. Or, else ...

I managed to cover it. By splitting the original certificate into three smaller ones. Two for $500,000 each and one for about $57,000. The difference went to cover the overdraft. That, was the best I could do. Legal or illegal.

But I remained without liquid cash. And I couldn't stop issuing checks. We issued some. Hoping to raise some cash in the meanwhile. Before they were presented for payment. But we couldn't make it. The Hanover Trust had to turn several down. An attorney for several investors, who for a week had been trying to round up some of my investors in order to petition for a receivership, saw his chance. He filed a petition in the bankruptcy courts. And that had the effect of stopping me from any further payments. Title to everything I had, automatically passed from me to the United States Courts.

It was the same night, I believe, that a city editor came up to my house in Lexington about midnight. Flashing a telegram from Montreal. But without allowing me to read It. Which wasn't necessary, anyway. Because I already had received my copy of it. He waved it at me and said that he had proofs of my Canadian conviction. Was going to print the story in the morning. Wanted to know whether I had anything to say.

"Yes, I have I told him." "You go ahead and print that story. But that will he the last issue of the paper that will ever be issued. You don't dare to print it. And you know it."

He didn't print it. He couldn't print it. The man from Montreal had wired him that, before he could be absolutely positive I was the same man who had been convicted in Canada, he would have to compare pictures. And so, I had another respite for a day or two. But the exposure was unavoidable.

Under the circumstances, the best I could do was to come out myself with the story. Before the newspapers did. So as to take the sting out.

I sent for Joe Toye. Then with the Boston Record. Now, city editor of the Boston Traveler. I told him the facts. Gave him my permission to use the story as soon as he had information that the papers were about to come out with. it. He used it. On the 11th, I believe.

My sole hope rested now in my ability to produce sufficient assets to meet my liabilities. Auditor Pride was about ready to report. And I was all set for the show-down. I had been down to the Hanover Trust. Picked out the securities I could use. Arranged for their temporary removal. And everything. But even that last hope failed to materialize.

Word reached me that the Bank Commissioner was up to something. I rushed down to the Hanover. And found the bank officials listening to an attorney. He was telling them that the Bank Commissioner intended to close the bank.

"What for?" I asked.

"Because he claims the bank's conditions are not sound," he replied.

"Not sound," interrupted one of the bank officials. "It's sounder now than it ever was. Our deposits have increased about 100% within the last two months."

"Well, maybe so," the attorney conceded, "but the Bank Commissioner insists that the bank has some bad loans on his books."

"You can tell him he is mistaken when he says that," I butted in. "This bank has not and cannot have any bad loans."

"Why?" asked the attorney.

"Because," I replied, "when I bought the control of this bank I went up to see the officials and told them that I would personally guarantee all loans. This bank holds a paper from me authorizing its officials to charge to my account any loan which may be deemed unsafe by the Bank Commissioner.'

"That's true," one of the bank officials confirmed. "We have that paper and the Bank Commissioner knows about it."

"Furthermore," I went on, "the Bank Commissioner told me when I bought the control of the Hanover that the bank was in sound condition. If it was then, it is still more so now. You go up to the State House and tell them what I told you. Tell them also that I still have over a million dollars in this bank to take care of the bad loans."

"I will go and see them," the attorney agreed. "After what you tell me, I am prepared to argue with him."

He went. Inside of half an hour he was back.

"Did you see them?" I asked him.

"I did," he replied.

"What did they have to say?" I inquired.

"They didn't say anything," the attorney stated. "They wouldn't say anything. He told me to see the Governor."

"And did you see the Governor?" I pressed him.

"I did," he answered. "And this is what he said: 'The Hanover must be closed'."

And the Hanover Trust Company was closed the same day. And then they got me.

The morning after, the 12th, I remained home. There was nothing I could do. But wait for things to happen. And happen they did.

First, Hermann called. I received him. And he exhibited a check for $10,000,000 made out to me. The check was certified to by the Harriman National Bank of New York. For a moment, the sight of that check rekindled my hopes. I asked him if he had the contract with him.

"No," replied Hermann. "I have not brought the contract. We have not changed our minds. But the latest developments have caused us to defer the matter for a couple of days."

"Oh, I see!" I remarked, using a commonplace expression. What I really meant was that I realized perfectly well the case of cold feet he had developed. Nevertheless, I made him stay with me and we chatted for a while.

Then, the telephone rang. I answered it. It was the United States Attorney. He asked me to go right down to his office because Pride was ready to report. I told Hermann that, if he cared to wait, he could. I had to go in town. I jumped in my car and went.

In the United States Attorney's office, I found, Mr. Assistant United States District Attorney, an auditor and one or two more people.

"Mr. Ponzi," said the Assistant United States District Attorney, "the auditor reports that the total of your outstanding liabilities is about $7,000,000. Are you ready to produce sufficient assets to cover them?"

"My liabilities are not $7,000,000," 1 replied. "I don't believe they are one-half of that sum."

"But you have agreed to accept the auditor's figures," he reminded me.

"Yes," I admitted. "I have agreed to accept his figures. Because I assumed, when I made the agreement, that his figures would not be more than a quarter of a million out of the way. Nevertheless, since I have agreed. I shall live up to the agreement."

"Are you ready to produce the assets?" the Assistant United States District Attorney insisted.

"Yes, I am," I told him. "But my total assets are of about $3,000,000."

"Then, you are $4,000,000 short," he remarked.

"I am," I conceded. "On the basis of the auditor's figures. Which I am precluded by my own agreement from disputing."

"Under the circumstances, I am sorry, Mr. Ponzi, but I must do my duty," he announced. "I must place you under arrest."

A United States deputy marshal stepped forward.

"Mr. Ponzi," he said, "in the name of the United States of America you are under arrest."

"O.K., marshal. I am your prisoner," I replied, making ready to follow him to the post-office and arrange about bail.

My house of cards had collapsed! The bubble had busted! I had lost! Lost everything! Millions of dollars. Credit.

Happiness. And even my liberty! Everything, except my courage. I needed that to take my medicine like a man. To meet the future. Unquestionably, I was licked. For the time being. But no man is ever licked, unless he wants to be. And I didn't intend to stay licked. Not so long as there was a flickering spark of life left in me. Like there was then. And there is now. Life, hope and courage are a combination which knows no defeat. Temporary set-backs, perhaps, but utter and permanent defeat, never!